# THE WAY OF NGO CHO KUN KUNG FU

## GRANDMASTER ALEXANDER LIM CO
### JUNE 12, 1953 – APRIL 12, 2016

# THE WAY OF NGO CHO KUN KUNG FU

Translated and Edited By
Alexander Lim Co

Under the Supervision of
Master Tan Kan Hong

www.TambuliMedia.com
Spring House, PA USA

DISCLAIMER

The author and publisher of this book DISCLAIM ANY RESPONSIBILITY over any injury as a result of the techniques taught in this book. Readers are advised to consult a physician about their physical condition before undergoing any strenuous training or dangerous physical activity. This is a martial arts book and details dangerous techniques that can cause serious physical injury and even death. Practice and training require a fit and healthy student and a qualified instructor.

First Published in 1983 by JAFAHA Publications (Binondo, Manila)
First Tambuli Media edition June 01, 2017

©1983, 2017

ISBN-13: 978-1-943155-25-5
ISBN-10: 1-943155-25-9

All Rights Reserved. No part of this publication may be reproduced or utilized in any form or by any means, electronic or mechanical, including photocopying, recording, or by any information storage and retrieval system, without prior written permission from the Publisher.

# FOREWORD TO THE 2017 EDITION

The late Grandmaster Alex Co was well-respected by the martial arts community at large. In the Philippines, his home country, he was known as "The Kung-fu Encyclopedia," for his vast knowledge on the subject. He is credited with many things, among which is having written and published the first two kung-fu books in the Philippines. The first was *The Secrets of Seven Star Praying Mantis* (JAHAFA 1981) followed by *The Way of Ngo Cho Kung Fu* (JAHAFA 1983).

I became Co Sifu's disciple in 1994 and became the first American sifu of Ngo Cho Kun as carried on through the Beng Kiam Athletic Club, of Binondo (Chinatown), Manila. It was in this year that Co Sifu presented me with the last printed copy of his dual-language (Chinese-English) book on Ngo Cho Kun (Five Ancestor Fist). In the decades that followed, Co Sifu and I did a second edition of this book through Tuttle Publishing (1997), titled *Five Ancestor Fist Kung-fu*, which included some additional information and replacement photos. This (also out of print) Tuttle edition has a blue cover while the original has a red cover; and so, we fondly refer to each book not by their respective titles, but by their cover colors! While the blue book is available on Kindle, the red book never saw a reprint and is of historical value and so we have faithfully republished the original dual-language book, with only few changes, to again make it available to enthusiasts and collectors.

In this Tambuli Media edition, we were able to re-scan many of the original photos. Unfortunately, many more have been lost over the decades and so some images are not as clear here as they were scanned from the original printing. We also added this foreword and some information in the back about our other books on the topic, and a new back cover. Otherwise, this is a faithful reproduction of the original volume.

Over the decades I spent with Co Sifu as his disciple, I can say we were also the best of friends. In addition to him training me, we spent so much time visiting old book shops, eating and laughing. I miss him dearly. I published several books and many magazine articles for Co Sifu, as well as arranging for and assisting in his 1998 Unique Publications video series on Ngo Cho Kun and Seven Star Mantis. And in his last years, with the help of Russ Smith, we were finally able to finish translating and publishing Yu Chiok Sam's rare and out of print book, *Chinese Gentle Art Complete* (Tambuli 2014), known within the art as "The Bible of Ngo Cho Kun."

In 1998, Beng Kiam entrusted me with heading up the American Beng Hong Athletic Club (named after Chua Giok BENG and Tan Ka HONG). In 2015, as Co Sifu's illness was taking its toll on him, I also became the disciple of Grandmaster Benito Tan, the son of Beng Kiam's founder, Sigong Tan Ka Hong. At this time, I was asked to expand Beng Hong into the International Beng Hong Athletic Association to become the international body for Beng Kiam's lineage.

This is all quite an honor for me. And it is my honor to bring Sigong Alex Co's original works back into print. I hope you enjoy them and that they influence you as they have me.

—*Dr. Mark V. Wiley*
Lansdale, PA - May 25, 2017
Publisher, Tambuli Media
President, International Bend Hong Athletic Association

# PREFACE

NGO CHO KUN (Five Ancestors Fist) is a Fukien Shaolin style consisting of techniques from five different styles namely WHITE CRANE (Fukien), MONKEY, TAI-CHO, LO HAN, TAT CHUN (Bodiharma). Founded by Sijo Chua Giok Beng in Chuan Chiu, Fukien China, it was brought over to the Philippines by Sigung Tan Kiong Beng, a direct disciple of the founder. For more than fifty years, it is being propagated by Sifu Tan Ka Hong (son of Sigung Tan Kiong Beng), second generation grandmaster, through the BENG KIAM ATHLETIC CLUB, the oldest kung fu school in the Philippines.

Being a martial arts enthusiast, my position as publisher and editor of MARTIAL ARTS MAGAZINE has allowed me the opportunity to meet different masters in their respective fields. As a collector of martial arts books with thousands of titles in English, Chinese and Japanese, I have learned the importance of these books in preserving the martial arts. To my knowledge there has been no good, authoritative book on the style of NGO CHO.

By fate, I was lucky enough to be able to study under different masters, acquiring sufficient knowledge of both Northern and Southern Shaolin, internal and external styles of kung fu. I was fortunate to be accepted as a student of NGO CHO kung fu under Sifu Tan Ka hong, the highest authority on the NGO CHO style in the Philippines.

This book was written with the permission and cooperation of Sifu Tan Ka Hong. His generous permission of allowing me to copy and translate from the "master text" (which is written in Chinese) handed down to him from his father is a great contribution to prospering and preserving the art of NGO CHO kung fu.

The Editorial Committee has helped in compiling materials for this book. I had the task of translating the master text into English. For a wider audience, I deemed the book to be published in Chinese with the corresponding English translation at each opposite page. Great efforts has been undertaken to render to the readers the most accurate translation. As some Chinese characters has no direct or accurate translation into English, I contended with the nearest interpretation and translation I can gather. I believe that the English Translations are clear enough for the interested practitioner.

I was also privileged to write the introduction for Sifu Tan Ka hong. I car say that this book is actually a labor of group coordination, and for all those who in one way or another has helped me to make this book possible, I extend my warmest gratitude.

## 福建五祖拳法序

　　中華武術，源遠流長，萌芽於狩獵，發端於戰爭，自我黃帝并創中華文化，垂今已五千多年矣，其間武術一道不斷衍化，派系日益繁多，乃有少林、武當、內外家、南北拳之分。在歷史上武術對於民族的生存競爭起着很大的作用，近百年來，由於火器發明，武術在戰爭中的地位日漸式微，但武術作為一項體育運動，可以健身，可以娛樂，可以自衛，可以衛人，在科學昌明的時代，仍不失其價值，武術被稱為國術，良有以也。

　　福建五祖拳法淵源於泉州，清咸豐年間，有晉江蔡玉鳴先生集太祖拳、羅漢拳、達尊拳、猴拳、白鶴拳之大成，綜合創編五祖拳法。一代宗師，垂法後世，門牆桃李，雲蒸霞蔚，遍及閩南各地，遠涉東南亞各國，至今已形成南少林一大流派。

　　余幼嗜技擊，拜五祖門名師陳家鴻老師門下習藝，承其厚愛，略識堂奧。本派同仁旅居菲島，數十年間，祖德宗功，未敢或忘，乃思滙集所學，留傳後世，因有「福建五祖拳法」一書刊行。余以為此書有益於發揚光大我中華武術，振奮中華民族尚武精神，福國利民，故樂而為之序。

洪樺羣　序
公元一九八三年六月

Benito Tan, Master Tan Ka Hong, Alfonzo Ang Hua Kun

# 福建五祖拳法
## The Way of Fukien Ngo Cho Kun Kung Fu

### 上篇　歷史
### PART I - HISTORY

第一章　福建五祖拳開宗祖師蔡玉鳴簡史
第二章　陳京銘師公簡史
第三章　簡介陳家鴻老師

Chapter 1 - History of NGO CHO KUN - Si jo Chua Giok Beng
Chapter 2 - Introduction to Sigung Tan Kiong Beng
Chapter 3 - Sifu Tan Ka Hong

### 中篇　拳法
### PART II TECHNIQUES

第四章　五肢力之運用
第五章　五祖拳法之馬步
第六章　五祖拳法之手肢

Chapter 4 - Ngo Ki Lat (Five-Parts Power)
Chapter 5 - Stances
Chapter 6 - Techniques:
    A. Hands
    B. Feet

第七章　五祖拳法全部拳套

Chapter 7 - Complete List of NGO CHO KUN-TO (Forms)
    A. The Basic Sam Chien
    B. Tamo's Method "Entwining Kick"
       "In Tit Tat"

㈠　五祖立法三戰
㈡　達尊法・茵藤踢

第八章　輪拳與械

Chapter 8 - Weapons

### 下篇　練功法
### PART III "LIAN KUNG WAT" Power Training Exercises

第九章　㈠　石鑽功
　　　　㈡　練掌功
　　　　㈢　五肢操手

Chapter 9  A. Chio-so Kung
        B. Palm Striking Exercises
        C. Ngo Ki Arm Hitting Exercises

Sitting on the middle Master Tan ka hong, kneeling on the left Alfonso Ang Hua Kun, kneeling on the right Alex Co.
Standing from left to right, Tan King Tong, Benito Tan, Bonifacio Lim, Willy Keh, Andy Ong, Leonardo Co, Henry Gan, Vicente Go.

## EDITORIAL STAFF

### 出版委員會

| | | | |
|---|---|---|---|
| Alexander Co | 許景偉 | 王安利 | Alexander Ong |
| Alfonso Ang Hua Kun | 洪樺羣 | 顏振城 | Henry Gan |
| Willy Keh | 郭德利 | 高慶新 | Bonifacio Lim |
| Leonardo Co | 許建寧 | 林司恩 | Perfecto Lim |
| Vicente Go | 吳新智 | 洪棋霖 | Johnny Ang |

中 坐 者：陳家鴻老師　　左跪者：洪樺羣　　右跪者：許景偉
從 左 至 右：陳慶堂（陳老師之長子）　陳少堂（陳老師之幼子）
　　　　　　高慶新　郭德利　王安利　許建寧　顏漢城　吳申智
不在像片者：林司恩　洪棋霖

# PART I - HISTORY OF NGO CHO KUN
## - SIJO CHUA GIOK BENG

# 上篇 歷史

## 第一章

## 福建五祖拳開宗祖師蔡玉鳴簡史

陳少堂

師祖蔡謙益字玉鳴。原名怡河。生於清末咸豐二年。公元一八五三年。世居泉州市南門外。離城十餘里。梅村坊尾鄉。世代經商。家財富裕。在漳州經營數家醬園。性好武術。天資聰敏。仗義疏財。不惜重金。禮聘各拳師傳授武功。其授業師傅鶴陽師。不幸染病亡故。他特親自扶鶴陽師靈柩。回河南原籍。旅途往返十載。沿路求師訪友。遍習各家各派拳藝。經過一番艱苦煅煉。十餘年浪跡江湖。會盡各家各派好手。更得福建少林寺高僧。傳授佛門外科醫術。有志者事竟成。其武功與日俱增。對南北各派武技。已爐火純青登峰造極。倦鳥思歸。一旦回到故鄉。青山依舊。人事已非。十多年浪跡江湖。其家產已花得一乾二淨。但他却不以為憂。反而落得清靜。遂將其一身所學之心得。集南北派拳術之艷技。共冶一爐。採取白鶴。太祖。羅漢。達尊。大聖五派之精華。綜合而成為白鶴指。齊天拳。太祖足。羅漢步。達尊身。獨出心裁。創設五祖拳法與諸般長短器械法。

師祖應武舉。原非本意。其在應試前。除拳術外。對於弓馬法。從未注意。原因泉州許多武舉紳士。仰慕其名氣。和他交誼。在許多武舉紳士慫恿下。才學弓馬法。一舉而中武秀才。其時已年近四十矣。晉南一帶。無不知其名氣。皆尊稱怡河師。或稱鳴老。但他素負大志。以清朝政治腐敗。大漢民族。為滿族所統治。無意進身仕途。一心創設武館。傳授門徒。並以精堪醫術。行醫濟世。

師祖精鐵沙掌。尤擅輕功提蹤。二丈高牆。一躍而上。故有枋尾之外號。名震福建全省。無人敢與之抗。其時八閩各地著名拳師。登門較技者。大不乏人。但都被其八法手所敗。斷羽而去。自是威名大振。門徒日眾。桃李遍八閩。在晉南五縣及漳廈一帶。稱為無敵。較有名氣拳師。都投其門下。學習五祖拳法。而他派拳師。亦因受五祖拳所影響。逐漸吸收五祖拳法。

師祖一生。授徒無數。其武館皆用仁義堂為館號。大門外楹聯亦有多款。但大都用「壯士來鉋三戰法。英雄且看五肢力」。在泉晉一帶。最著名者。有泉晉五祖拳十虎。即泉州林九如師。官橋尤祝三 魏文豹「又名翻天豹」。落地金鮫孤程的師。賣油條粱師。鳳尾手何海師。陳魁師。青陽鴻矯師。柯彩雲師。陳京銘師。號金翼大鵬。為師祖衣鉢弟子。

師祖好交江湖朋友。三教九流。如有一技之長。登門求助。無不以禮相待。留食留宿。其住宅建土樓一座。不設門戶。武林中人。如擅輕功者。一躍上樓。則待以上賓。至今土樓。雖年久損壞。但舊址仍存。其鄉人還保存着對他歌頌楹聯一對曰。「玉尺量材世見稀」。「鳴鐘起舞夜聞雞」。在閩南民間。「有滿路香」之綽號。原因他門徒眾多。各地爭相延聘。所以到處都受歡迎款待。晚年時候。由於有眾多門徒關懷照顧。已不愁食不愁穿。他一向重義輕利。生活儉樸。長年只穿藍布長衫一條。盡管門徒奉獻上好四季衣裳。總不見他穿用。原來他將新衣穿在裏面。外面仍穿着那一件舊布長衫。如遇窮苦者求助。便將新衣脫下贈給人家。

師祖在民間。行俠仗義之事蹟甚多。未能盡述。一生淡泊明志。如閒雲野鶴。其武功武德。皆足為後人斥式。誠一派開宗之祖耳。

PART I - History

# CHAPTER - 1  EARLY YEARS OF THE NGO-CHO (Go-Cho) Style: FOUNDER SIJO CHUA GIOK BENG

The roots of the NGO CHO KUN traces back to Sijo Chua Kiam, alias Giok Beng, also named I-Ho of Fukien, China. Chua Giok Beng was born in 1853, amidst the turmoil of the declining years of the Ching Dynasty. He lived in the village of Pan Be, a few miles away from the city of Chuan Chiu. Belonging to a wealthy family, his parents are principally engaged in the sauce manufacturing business. They have what is called a sauce garden, a place where salty Chinese foods are manufactured by immersing and then draining the foods in salty sauce. With the prosperous outlook of their business, brightening up through the years, still Giok Beng's heart and soul has always been in the practice of kung fu. To him, material fulfillment and gain is secondary, his kung fu being the top priority. This intense desire to learn the kung-fu arts drove him to avail of the kung-fu expertise of Master Ho Yang. The venue of the instruction is the sauce garden of Chua Giok Beng, thus enabling him to utilize his time dually: practising his craft while at the same time overseeing his business.

Chua Giok Beng's master eventually died of old age, and loyal as a disciple, he attended personally to the funeral rites of his old master. He escorted the old master's remains back to the latter's place in Honan China.

The following ten years that ensued saw Chua Giok Beng searching and learning other styles of kung-fu. He learned the art of Chinese medicine from a high priest of one of Fukien province's Shaolin temples. In his more than ten years of zealous searching, learning and perfecting the kung-fu arts, he was able to absorb the best techniques of the Northern and Southern Shaolin styles. When he felt that his expertise is already at its zenith, he journeyed back home only to be surprised and depressed at the sad state of his once lucrative business. Not to be completely overtaken by his business losses, he decided to concentrate on his kung-fu, his first love. With enough time in his hands, he was able to fuse together the excellent styles derived from his more than ten years of zealous training. He grouped together the techniques of Pe-Ho (White Crane), Tai-Cho (Emperor Sung), Lohan (Arhat), Tat Chun (Bodiharma) and Tai Sheng (Monkey). He later categorized his movements into the following: Peho-Che (Finger Strikes of White Crane), Che Tian Chiong (Palm Techniques of the Monkey), Tai Cho Ka (Kicking Techniques of Emperor Sung Tai Cho), Lo Han Pu (Steps of the Lo-Han), Tat Chun Sin (Body Postures of Tamo). From these, he eventually came up with a pierce, powerful style, the NGO-CHO Kun, or GO-CHO style of kung-fu (Five Ancestor Fists).

Chua Giok Beng later on infused in his style the use of different kinds of weapons.

His expertise in kung-fu reached greater heights, and he was treated with respect and esteem throughout Chuan Chiu. He earned the monicker I-Ho or Meng Lo (Wise Beng) because of his knowledge. By insistent proddings from kung-fu enthusiasts, he began to teach his kung-fu to trusted disciples and eventually opened his own kung-fu shcool. He also made use of his superrb knowledge in medicine, offering his doctoral services to the community.

Sijo Chua Giok Beng was also an expert in the Iron Palm and Kin Gung (light body techniques). He could effortlessly leap up to a two-storey house with a single jump. With his amazing acrobatic feat, he became known as Pan Be Ho (The Crane of Pan Be Village). In his heydays, his name ringed a bell throughout Fukien. Other masters were soon intrigued by his tremendous popularity that many challenged him. They were defeated by Beng's deadly Pat Wat (Eight-Method Deadly Techniques). Many of those who challenged him and doubted his knowledge in kung-fu later on became his students, infusing and integrating in their former styles the salient features of the Ngo Cho Kun learned from Giok Beng.

Giok Beng formed his club and named it Lin Gi Tong. On its door hanged a couplet which read: "Gentlemen, let us study the way of Sam Chien and warrior, please observe my Ngo Ki Lat (Five Parts Power).

In his place, Chuan Chiu, Giok Beng's finest students became known as the "Ten Tigers of NGO CHO KUN". They were:

1. Kiu Lu of Chuan Chiu known as Kao Sai
2. Yu Chiok Sam of Kuan Kio
3. Wei Bun Pa known as Wan Tian Pa
4. Lok Te Kim Kao
5. Bicho Seller
6. Phoenix Hand Ho Hai Sai
7. Tan Tao Sai
8. Hong Kiao Sai of Ching Yong
9. Kua Chai Hun Sai
10. Tan Kiong Beng Sai alias Golden Wings Tai Peng

Being very famous, Giok Beng made many friends from all walks of life. Almost anyone who has a special ability in the kung-fu arts is welcomed to stay in his house as his guest. His house in Pan Be has no doors, only windows, and anyone who has good kung-fu and can jump from the ground to his house is welcomed as an honored guest. His house in fact remain up to this day in Chuan Chiu.

Chua Giok Beng was also given the nickname Mua Lo Hiong (popular all the way) due to his overwhelming popularity. In his later years, he became a nomadic, constantly moving and roaming from one place to another. He led the life of a hermit, and simplicity became his rule for the day. He would garb himself in almost raggedy like clothes, and his disciples would give him new clothes or money. Not that they were pitying him as you would pity a beggar, but it was just their way of compensating him for the knowledge they got from him. Unperturbed by any material desires, he would give away his new clothes to the destitute he meets on the way, making him a sort of philanthropist in his own way.

# CHAPTER II - INTRODUCTION TO SIGUNG TAN KIONG BENG

師公陳京銘之遺像
號稱「金翼大鵬」

# 第二章　　陳京銘師公簡史

### 許 建 寧

　　陳京銘師公。號大鵬。世居福建泉州市。南門義全舖。為泉城富商。體魄魁梧雄偉天生神力。能舉五百斤石獅。性好武。廿歲以弓馬入泮。為人仗義好友。揮金如土。禮聘名震福建五祖拳宗師蔡玉鳴。傳授五祖拳法。以其天資聰穎。臂力過人。甚得師祖痛愛。當時師祖在泉州一帶。綽號「滿路香」。很多富商巨賈。爭相延聘。所以無法將師祖長久留在家中。但學藝心切。藝未成不能中輟。不得不追隨師祖。四方奔走。十餘年勤修苦練。盡得五祖拳全部精髓。尤擅鐵沙掌絕枝。及外科跌打醫術。被稱為五祖拳十虎之一。橋手堅硬。其一招大鵬展翼手。所向無敵。

　　師公在泉州市。所設醫館。師祖賜號曰仁億堂。除行醫濟世。並無授徒。只傳授族中少數子弟。而已。為人富俠義。謙虛抑己。抱濟世之雄心。義務拾醫拾藥。嘗謂大丈夫生於亂世。不能以身許國。亦應將所學貢獻人羣。

　　公元一九一八年。數次南渡旅遊菲律濱。其生前不論在國內國外。皆以行醫濟世。義舉遠播。但淡泊名利。在菲賓亦只收門徒十餘人。生平古道熱腸。修養功深。武德醫德。皆為俊人所敬仰者耳。

## CHAPTER II - THE IST GENERATION MASTER: Sigung Grandmaster Tan Kiong Beng

Grandmaster Tan Kiong Beng is a first generation master of NGO CHO kun who received personal instruction from its founder Chua Giok Beng. Nicknamed Tai Peng, he was born in Chuan Chiu, Fukien, China, to a wealthy, business oriented family. Being very muscular and gifted with a strong physigue, he could easily lift a stone sculptured lion weighing 500 lbs. a considerable distance from the ground. Fond of the martial arts, he tried his luck for the "Bushiu Chai", a military officer slot, by hurdling the examinations with flying colors: the examinations required him to shoot arrows to a certain target while he is astride a running horse. This feat he was able to accomplish at a young age of twenty.

During those times, it was customary for rich families to hire the services of kung-fu experts to teach in their mansions. Normally, rich families hire the most noted kung fu practitioner of the moment. At that time, Sijo Chua Giok Beng was the most noted kung-fu player and he was hired by Tan Kiong Beng's family as their private tutor. Tan Kiong Beng's family was highly privileged and honored to have Giok Beng as their private instructor. Added to this is the fact that Tan Kiong Beng is a noted man of good moral character which befits him to be a direct in-door disciple of Chua Giok Beng. Though he learned enough of what Giok Beng knew, still Tan Kiong felt he needed more. He followed Giok Beng in the latter's sojourn throughout China and persevered to absorb the complete mastery of Ngo Cho kun. After more than ten years of continuous, devoted training, Sigung Tan Kiong Beng became a master. Under the tutorship of Master Beng, he became adept in the iron palm and became widely acknowledged for his expertise in the "Tai Peng" (Roc) "spreading its wings" technique where he was unbeatable. With his proficiency in the arts, he was given due recognition as one of the "Ten Tigers of Ngo Cho Kun".

Aside from Sigung Tan Kiong Beng's expertise in the martial arts, he is also knowledgeable in Chinese medicine. He opened his own clinic in Chuan Chiu, and master Giok Beng blessed him with the authority to name his clinic "Lin Tek Tong", after the old master's own club. Like his master Giok Beng, Sigung Tan Kiong's first love was kung-fu. He practised often and whatever time is left he devoted to his clinic. He taught only his closest friends though many were after his knowledge. To him, the quality of his students is better than the quantity.

Sometimes in 1918, Sigung Tan Kiong Beng visited the Philippines and offered his services as a doctor to his fellow overseas Chinese-Filipino friends and acquaintances. His knowledge in the NGO CHO arts did not pass unnoticed even among local kung fu enthusiasts and prompted by numerous proddings from eager friends, he taught his art to a selected few. His skills in the NGO CHO style as well as in Chinese medicine is still being vividly remembered up to this day.

Taken in 1937. Officers of the Bengkiam Club with master Tan Ka Hong prior to his trip back to China (2nd from left)
Sitting on the center Sijuk Cho Chang Hun Chiong, Honorary President, 2nd from right Lim Tian Suy President.

Sifu Tan Ka Hong

# 第三章　簡介陳家鴻老師

### 許景偉

　　陳家鴻老師。世居福建泉州市。乃父陳京銘師公。家境殷厚。素習武事。少以弓馬入泮。追隨五祖拳宗師蔡玉鳴師祖。練習五祖拳法。為師祖衣缽弟子。盡得五祖法精髓。師公繼室王太夫人。為晉江白鶴派名拳師王溪生愛女。得家傳白鶴拳法。

　　陳家鴻老師。幼受庭訓。七歲入學攻書。並隨母學習白鶴拳。十一歲京銘師公。開始傳授五祖拳。十餘年苦練。盡得五祖拳之精華。後以因緣巧合。得江西少林分寺。俗家弟子金占鰲師。傳授少林派槍刀劍棍。諸般器械法。身兼數家武功。

　　京銘師公。早年曾經數渡旅遊菲律濱。以師祖所傳醫術。在菲行醫濟世。活人無數。

公元一九三四年。南京中央國術館館長。張之江。爲提倡國術。宣揚國粹。率領國術隊。到南洋各埠。宣揚表演武術。順途到菲律濱。作數場演出。甚得僑胞歡迎。當時張雲章師叔祖。亦率領師公舊門徒十人。客串參加表演五祖拳法。頗獲僑界人仕讚許。

張雲章先生。前清秀才。亦是師祖入室弟子。文武雙全。於民初應聘來菲任岷里拉中西學校校長。因此倡議再聘請京銘師公。重臨菲島。傳授五祖拳。但師公以年近古稀。想要在家多享幾年清福。無意再遠涉重洋。但諸門徒函電交馳。殷殷懇請。亦以五祖拳法。須發揚光大。不能由此湮沒。故特命家鴻老師。代父南渡。陳老師以父命難違。不得不束裝就道。遠走異邦。離家前一晚。在師祖神前拈香立誓。（一）要發揚光大五祖拳法。（二）要遵守師祖戒律。（三）要以溫良恭儉讓爲處世待人之道。遂於公元一九三五年春。買掉波菲。

雲章師叔祖。及數位師伯師叔。於歡迎宴後。組籌備會。討論組社事宜。並討論社之名稱。當經雲章師叔祖提議。本派五祖拳法。爲師祖蔡玉鳴所創設。師祖諱謙字玉鳴。爲紀念師祖創設五祖拳法之偉大精神。命名爲菲律濱中華鳴謙國術社。

公元一九三八年。中華鳴謙國術社慶祝成立三週年紀念。雲章師叔祖曾題讚詞曰。先師諱謙。一字玉鳴。武科領峻。國術尤精。南柔北勁。集其大成。神龍夭矯。久著成名。公門桃李。隨地向榮。人雖西去。道猶南行。薪傳妙技。播及海濱。師恩不遠。永留英靈。

公元一九四五年岷市光復。但毀於炮火。支離破碎。滿目瘡痍陳老師力倡復社。多方奔走。於翌年一九四六年十月間。自建堂皇社所一座。鳴謙社之基礎。更加鞏固。

日月如梭。轉眼間鳴謙國術社。已經過四十八週年。社務更加欣欣向榮。訓練並無間斷。此皆得自歷屆理事長。曁諸理監事通力合作。努力倡導。數十年來爲聯絡中菲友誼。提倡體育。運動。有百場向外宣揚表演。陳老師除授徒外。兼以師祖所授外科跌打。移輪接骨醫術。服務人羣。待人和藹可親。俊恭有禮。對門徒諄諄善誘。雖已年近八十高齡。精神矍鑠。雄風不減壯年。今者五祖拳法。照遍全菲。門徒遍及全菲各角落。皆陳老師苦心培植。才有今日之成就。

# CHAPTER -III PRESENT DAY 2ND GENERATION GRANDMASTER:
## Sifu Tan Ka Hong

Sifu Tan Ka Hong is the present day forerunner of the NGO CHO style of kung-fu not only in the Philippines but in Asia as well. He is the son of Sifu Tan Kiong Beng, who is an in-door disciple of the Ngo Cho founder, Master Chua Giok Beng. To whom can Master Sigung Tan Kiong Beng bequethed his precious knowledge than to one of his own flesh and blood?

Sifu Tan Ka Hong grew up in a family embedded with kung-fu influences and traditions. Aside from having a father who is an expert in the Go-Cho style, he also has for a mother a White Crane stylist. His mother is a daughter of Fukien White Crane master Ong Kue Seng.

Sifu Tan Ka Hong learned the rudiments of kung-fu at an early age through the patient teaching of his mother. At the age of seven, his mother taught him techniques of the White Crane. He divided his time between schooling and studying kung-fu. When he reached eleven years of age, his father started teaching him the Ngo Cho style under a strict regimen. After more than ten years of sweating it out with the Ngo Cho style, he gained complete mastery of the art, including the very important secretive art of Chinese medicine.

He eventually met Master Kim Chian, a disciple of Shaolin kungfu who later taught him the techniques of the Shaolin and varied weaponry like the sword, staff, spear, knife, etc., thus widening his kung-fu horizons to include both the Northern and Shaolin kung-fu styles, a perfect blend of arts complementing each other.

Recorded exploits of the Ngo Cho style are very few, but highly impressive. In 1934, the president of the Nanking Central Kung Fu Institute Chang Tze Chiang went with a group of kung fu experts to Manila in order to promote kung fu through exhibitions and dialogues with various kung fu clubs. Ngo Cho Master Sijuk Cho Chang Hun Chiong together with some old students of Sigung Tan Kiong Beng participated as guest performers in the kung fu exhibition and the local audience for the first time was treated to the astounding power of the GO-CHO arts.

Sijuk Cho Chan Hun Chiong was a scholarly man, aside from being a kung-fu expert. Being an in-door desciple of Sijo Chua Giok Beng, he was able to absorb the styles and techniques of the old master. Other than this, academic excellence is his second motivation in life. He came over to Manila to assume the principal's seat at the Tiong Se Academy. Though he revolves within the academe, still his skills in the martial arts did not remain unnoticed. Because of the warm reception and interests shown by martial artists to the Ngo Cho style, he was deeply inspired at the prospect of opening a Go-Cho club. He wrote Sigung Tan Kiong Beng and presented him with the bright prospects of opening up a club in the Philippines at the same time inviting the old sifu to come over to the Philippines and spearhead the Ngo-Cho arts in the country. Sigung Tan Kiong Beng, because of old age, felt he does not have to go to the Philippines personally. Demonstrating his complete trust in Sifu Tan Ka Hong who learned everything he knew, Sifu Beng sent Tan Ka Hong to the Philippines to fulfill the task offerred him. The night of the eve of his departure, the elder Beng made Sifu Tan Ka Hong swear before the altar to observe the following in his teaching the Ngo-Cho arts: a) prosper the art of Go-Cho; 2) respect and follow the rules and tenets of the style; 3) to always treat people with respect, humility of character, excercise morality and fulchritude at all times.

In 1935, Sifu Tan Ka Hong arrived in Manila to fullfill his task and he was warmly received by Sijukcho Chang Han Chiong, together with some of Sigung Tan King Beng's students.

The organization of a kung-fu club was immediately discussed. Sijukcho Chang Han Chiong suggested that since Sijo was known as Chua Giok Beng, they might as well name the club Beng Kiam in memory and respect to its founder, thus perpetuating the grand old man's name to posterity.

After the war in 1945, Manila was left in ruins and the formerly active Beng Kiam Club needed resuscitation. Sifu Tan Ka Hong gathered together the people devoted in the Ngo-Cho arts and set up again the Beng Kiam Athletic Club. Beng Kaim eventually was able to build its own house, definitely planting its roots here in the Philippines.

Forty eight years had elapsed and Beng Kiam is still the name to reckon with as far as local kung fu clubs is concerned. It has turned out hundreds of students with the able support of its directors under the supervision of Master Tan Ka Hong. Its students have spread to other parts of Asia, some making it to the United States and other far-away countries.

The Bengkiam house still stands today. Though already old, Bengkiam's interior bespeaks of ancient Chinese kung fu traditions what with the Chinese altar at its center, plus the swords and varied weaponry at the sides.

Through the years, Bengkiam has demonstrated goodwill among local Chinese and Filipinos through kung fu exhibitions and demonstrations. Aside from this, Master Tan Ka Hong similarly offerred his knowledge of herbal/Chinese medicine to the local Chinese community.

Sifu Tan Ka Hong in his capacity as a master is close to his students and treats them with kindness and fatherly concern, very much like the Chinese tradition of strict master-disciple relationship.

Sifu Tan Ka Hong is already in his eighties, witnessing the eight decades of kung-fu's ups and downs in China and the Philippines. His agility, clearness of sight, excellence in hearing and solid countenance bespeaks of what a real master should be. Indeed, his age has not betrayed him, after all. And all these because he holds the secrets of staying young, in this case not a secret anymore: just plain, real, honest-to-goodness kung fu.

Master Tan Ka Hong with Son Benito Tan

Members of the Beng Kiam Club with Master Tan Ka Hong (seated 3rd from left) in 1937.

# PART II  TECHNIQUES

二十拳團體表演　Group Demonstration of Lisipkuan (Twenty punches) taken in 1975

# 中篇拳法

## 第四章　五肢力之運用

### 郭　德　利

師祖傳拳之道。曰氣。曰勢。曰力。三者備而精乎其技。精氣神三者全則力生。

夫拳術者。首重姿勢。無姿勢則如傀儡登場。雖亦步亦趨。旅進旅退。則淹然而無生氣耳。是故其行拳也。勢踏戰馬。不丁不八。前四後六。「即前腳四分力。後腳六分力。」馬坐後肢。搶大椎以通中氣。兜前足而固膀胱。兩肩墜而心胸守。拳握半陰半陽。樹由根基起。力從足底生。耳能聽風眼光四顧。伏如處女。動如脫冤。是皆五祖之姿勢也。

若論五肢之力。頭頂天平硬正。骸下地閣直墜牙關起如鵝啼。聲音發似虎吼。魁星臂練魚目。舌托上。鼻如獅。手有三節力分三池部位。三池對肩胛。兩胛須齊墜。上節沉肩。中節吞吐。尾節如龍戲水。出手吐氣。收手吸氣。以氣摧力。搖肩駿胛。欲發先收。發力有聲。即是內勁。內堅如鐵。外柔如棉。剛柔相濟。身如車輪轉動。腹似鐵壁堅硬。前三部。提膀胱。起丹田。獻八卦。後三部。落大臂。束腰力。插尾尻。

夫馬勢多毅。慎自靈敏。足有三節力。陰根提起。陽根降落。頂腿夾入。膝眼展開。五指收起。腳心吸落。自然步步生根。落地不移。宛如銅牆鐵壁。鍛鍊精純。自能得心應手耳。

# CHAPTER - IV - APPLICATION OF NGO KI LAT (FIVE PARTS POWER)

The Sijo in his way of teaching the NGO CHO style put emphasis on chi (ki; breath), sze (form), li (strength). If these three qualities are cultivated to perfection, then your kung-fu will be very excellent. By combining ching, chi, shen (spirit, breath and soul), then power will come very easily.

The NGO CHO style of kung fu put its emphasis on sze (form). Without the proper form, then the practitioner is just like a puppet being pulled and controlled by a string. Lacking the proper form, the practitioner moving forward and backward lacks the grace and posture of his style. In the NGO CHO style, proper form is not only necessary but it is also a must. To start with, he should assume the proper stance (chien-be) which is either T shaped or 入 shaped.

In the stance, one leg is forward and the other is backward. The weight is distributed thus: 40% on the front; 60% on the back. (i. e., 40% of the weight is on the front leg; 60% is on the back leg) Thus, the saying "4 on the front; 6 on the back"

The weight of the stance is concentrated on the back leg, then by sinking in the buttocks, it allows the spinal column to form a straight line from the tip of the head, thus forming a straight pathway for the easy passing of chi. As the stance have knees drawn inward than outward, the upper extremities are likewise tensed driving the male testicles upward than its usual level. Constant practice on this will automatically place the testicles upward, protecting/shielding it. The testicles no longer is drooping; it is "hiding". No other style of kung fu has such a unique training style which predominantly concerns the male organ.

While in the stance, the shoulder are drooped so as to sink the chest in. Not that one should assume the huncback posture. The shoulder blades are out, while the chest is in. This develops the strength of the lower portions of the back while at the same time adding flexibility to the shoulders.

The fist or punch is half ying, half yang (halfway between horizontal and vertical).

The feet should hold the practitioner firmly to the ground. Just as the foundation of a tree come from its roots, the source of his strength should emanate from the soles of his feet.

The ears should be sharp to detect even the slightest blowing of the wind.

The eyes should be aware of the four directions to the human gate: left and right; back and front.

The above characteristics are present if you assume the right form (se) of NGO CHO kun. Motionless, the practitioner serenely manifests the gentleness of a lady, actively projects the agility of a rabbit.

## THE NGO KI LAT (Five-Parts Power)

The NGO KI LAT (Five-Parts Power) of GO CHO KUNG refers to the head, hands and feet. The hands as a source of power requires rigid training, like the other parts of the body. The head should be upright, the chin sunk low, the mouth open as if in a "gay smile"; the front teeth piercely gritting against each other simulating the form of a crying rooster; the inhalation-exhalation simulating the ferocity of a tiger. This "toothsome smile" is to be held while doing the drills, helping the practitioner to tense his neck. To complete the fierce look, the eyes are held wide open, like the eyes of a big fish. Inside the mouth, the tongue is curled up to the upper palate. The muscles at the sides of the lips are tensely pulled to the sides of the neck, the nostrils simultaneously expanded. With a single look, the practitioner, in such a state of face contortions looks like a beast ready to grab its prey. The air seems to produce the quiet sound of a tamed but pierce growl of a tiger with the alternate inhalation/ exhalation. To complete the picture, the nostrils are expanded like that of a ferocious lion.

The power source of the hands embraces the shoulders and the upper torso, aside from the hands and arms. The power source of the hands can be roughly divided into three parts: The first part refers to the shoulder area. The shoulders should be drooped, sinking the chest in. Feel the weight going down the buttocks. The second or middle part refers to the elbow: the sides of the elbows are tucked in at the sides while the portion from the elbow up to the wrists are extended with the fingers pointing upward to the ceiling. When the hands are thrusts forward and backward, with the shoulders drooped and the forearms tucked to the sides, the hands will vibrate due to the tensing of the muscles. In Chinese, they likened this force to a "dragon playing in the water". Exhale when you thrust your hands forward, inhale when you retract your hands to your sides. With the continued inhalation and exhalation use chi to produce power or strength. Twist/shake the shoulders and tremble the stomach. Before thrusting the hands out, pull them in to gain momentum so that when you thrust them out, there will be a vibrating sound of your strength. This vibrating sound is nei-ching (intrinsic energy). Internally, you're hard as steel, but externally and physically, you're soft as cotton, maintaining an equilibrium or hard and soft. The body, though hard and flexible, is like a wheel when turning. The stomach is hard as a steel wall. The frontal three parts of the body are thus: the testicles tucked in, with concentration focused on the tan tien; the chest (pakua) expanded; and the three parts at the back: tensely lower your hips, tighten the waist and seemingly tuck in the tip of the spinal column (cocyx) to make it form a straight line from the head to the buttocks, for the easy passage of chi in the body.

The third part power souce are the feet. When in a stance, the legs should be firmly held to the ground to achieve stability. The stance should be fast and agile. The feet's power source comprises of three segments: the upper legs or thighs, the lower legs, and the feet. In practising the three parts, you should will your mind to have chi circulating through inhalation and exhalation, with chi passing from one leg to another as if in a continuing cycle. In the three segments of the legs, the thighs are tucked in, the ankles exposed out, then the toes are curled up to tense the calf muscles, with the soles of the feet glued to the ground. With the proper form, automatically every step will be firm like roots sunken to the ground, forming a very firm stance, making one like a steel wall. Diligent practice will enable one to move with ease and coordination.

# 第五章　五祖拳法之馬步

## 吳　新　智

煆煉五祖拳法有腰馬穩固力實勢猛之特點其馬步法有。
丁八馬卻戰馬　八字馬　四平馬　角馬　弓箭馬　左弓右箭馬。　右弓左箭馬直進步　直退步　踏步　疊進步　疊退步　閃馬步　榻馬步　閃榻步　屈馬步　跳進步　跳退步　旋螺跳步　寄足步　左穿梭步　右穿梭步

## CHAPTER - V  STANCES

In practicing NGO CHO kun, its special characteristics, strength and ferocity, require the stability of its stance. The following are the stances of NGO CHO kun:

1. T ( 八 ) shaped stance or the chian be - weight is distributed 40% on the front leg, 60% on the back leg. This is the most commonly used stance of the NGO CHO, and the basis of all footworks.

2. Level horse stance - the two knees seem to be meeting opposite each other with weight distribution of both legs equal.

3. Corner stance - this is the chian be stance executed at the sides

4. Bow and arrow stance - weight is distributed 70% on the front leg, 30% on the back leg. Commonly known in karate as the front stance. This stance could be further subdivided into the left or right bow and arrow stance.

1

2
LEVEL HORSE STANCE

4
BOW AND ARROW

# NGO CHO FOOTWORKS (STEPS)

The NGO CHO style utilizes short steps in moving about. The steps may be short and swift but actually they carry such force that can crash a head. The following are the different footworks (steps) of NGO CHO kun:

1. Direct forward step - From the chian be stance, step forward with your right leg, the left leg drags behind

2. Direct backward step - this time, instead of stepping forward, you step backward.

3. Step on - from the stance, move one foot either forward or backward.

4. Double Forward step - from the chian be stance, move left foot forward, then right foot forward.

5. Double backward step - from number 4, do the procedure backwards, instead of forward

**DIRECT FORWARD STEP**

6. Evading step - step either to your left or right to evade.

7. Overlapping step - left foot passes or crisscrosses over the right, then step with your right leg sideways. This is similar to the double step, only here you crisscrosses.

8. Evading overlap step - move by overlapping step either to the left or right

9. Crouched kneeling step - move your feet to achieve the half kneel position

10 Jumping forward - jump forward to attack

11. Jumping backward - jump backwards to evade

12. Spiral turning jump - twist in mid-air 360o

13. Hanging leg step - similar to toe stance; effective in evading and closing in.

14. Left and right crouched stance- extend one leg out and bend low to the ground. Weight is 70% on the crouched leg, 30% on the extended one. This movement is done usually in preparation fro the scissor kick

STEP ON

BOW & ARROW STANCE

**DOUBLE FORWARD STEP**

OVERLAPPING STANCE

**HANGING LEG STEP**

**CROUCHED KNEELING STEP**

# CHAPTER VI - TECHNIQUES
## A. HANDS
## B. FEET

# 第六章　五祖拳法之手肢

## 洪樺羣

手法之動作。占拳術上重要部份。因拳術為手上功夫。包羅拳掌指各部在內。各宗派手法之多。譬南山之竹。不能盡書。然而無論何派手法之動作。不外高挑。平衝。低砍。直劈。擒拿。點戳。虛實吞吐而已。善用其手者。出沒無常。循環變化。或挑或格。或砍或劈。同吞出吐。虛實莫測。使敵眼花神亂。無從遮掩。遂我手到成功。五祖拳法之手肢。共分為。

　單手長肢攻法。　　單手長肢解法。
　雙手長肢攻法。　　雙手長肢解法。
　單手短肢攻法。　　單手短肢解法。
　雙手短肢攻法。　　雙手短肢解法。
　下盤屈馬攻法。　　下盤屈馬解法。

五祖拳之手法。共二百五十招式。總之格拒招攔。轉圜如意。起落迅速。來去如風。運用如此。方臻其妙。

## THE HAND TECHNIQUES OF NGO CHO KUN

The hands play a major part in kung-fu principally because kung-fu is a pugilistic art. The hands refer to the palm, fist, and fingers. Every style of kung-fu has its own unique hand techniques, and it is a gigantic task, if not outright impossible, to condense the different hand techniques into a book. But whatever styles we are referring to, it is considered a basic fact that the major movements of the hands are to deflect upward, thrust forward, hook downward, to chop (straight split); grab hold, hit and cut, extend and retract. For the practitioner who has mastered his hand techniques, he may make his hand movements unpredictable by continuously interchanging his techniques, i. e., by either deflecting, hooking, blocking or splitting (chopping), thrusting and retracting, or combination attack-block-attack. His movements may be real or just feints, thus confusing the opponent, making him unable to tell the real from the fake (feint) movements. This confusion will catch his enemy off-guard and the able practitioner could easily close in and deliver his intended blow.

1　2

## 五祖拳法之肢手

### （一）單手長肢攻法

① 右衝拳－拳握半陰半陽，用拳撞擊敵人胸部。
② 右手掌釵－用手掌邊緣擊敵人胸部。
③ 右切手－用右手掌邊緣擊敵人之腰側。
④ 青龍點－用右拳擊敵人左太陽穴。
⑤ 右手虎爪－用右手掌擋敵人胸部。

**HAND TECHNIQUES OF THE NGO CHO KUN**

1. SINGLE LONG HAND TECHNIQUES (Attack)

   A)  Straight Punch - The hand position is half ying, half yang, which means neither verticle nor horizontal.

   B)  Side Straight Chop - Use the right side of the palm to strike/chop your opponent's chest.

   C)  Slice Chop - Use the right side of the palm to straight thrust into your opponent's waist.

3   4

D) Green Dragon Spot - Roundhouse punch: Hit your opponent's left temple

E) Right Tiger Claw - Use the palm to thrust

5

1　　　　2

（二）雙手長肢攻法

① 雙龍點頭—用左右拳擊敵人左右太陽穴。
② 孩兒抱牌式—用左右掌推擋敵人胸及腹部。
③ 雙掛手—用左右雙掌直擋敵人胸部。
④ 雙壁拳—用左右手雙拳直撞敵人心及胸部。
⑤ 雙批左畔—用左右雙掌邊綠擊敵人左腰側，並用左脚掃敵人左脚。

2. DOUBLE LONG HAND TECHNIQUES (Attack)

   A) Double Dragon Spot to the Head - Double round house punch to opponent's temple

   B) The Child Holding the Table - Strike out with your palms, the left palm at the chest and the right palm at the abdomen

   C) Double Palm Strike - Strike out with both palms, bending sideways, aiming at your opponent's chest.

3  4

D) Double Straight Punch - Punch both fists into the center aimed at your opponent's heart and stomach.

E) Double Chop - Raise both palms to your right side, and chop down with the right palm facing upward, the left palm facing downward and sweep with your left foot as it goes forward

5A  5B

1　　　　2

（三）單手短肢攻法
① 右手拳損―擊敵人心胸部。
② 右擒手―擊敵人丹田下。
③ 右鞭手―擊敵人面中。
④ 啄手―右手掌啄擊敵人胸部。
⑤ 鳳鼓劈―劈擊敵人面部。


3) SINGLE SHORT HAND TECHNIQUES (Attack)

  A)   Right Hammer Strike - Strike down with your right fist towards your opponent's chest

  B)   Right Uppercut - Strike upward uppercutting into your opponent's lower abdomen

  C)   Right Backfist (Whip) Strike - Strike down with your backfist into your opponent's face

3

4

5

D) Finger strike
E) Downward chop

1　　　2

（四）雙手短肢攻法

① 抱偏右—側擊推擋敵人身體右側邊。
② 雙擠手—雙拳擠擊敵人下腹。
③ 雙貫拳—雙拳擊敵人丹田及下腹。
④ 鉤搖手—左手鉤開敵人右手，右拳擠擊敵人下腹。
⑤ 雙開剪—左右拳雙開剪斷敵人左拳。

4). DOUBLE SHORT HAND TECHNIQUES (Attack)

A) Po-pian (holding the side) - Strike to your right with your left palm, and strike out with the side of your fist in a phoenix fist position to your right aimed at your opponent's kidney.

B) Double Uppercut - With both fists, uppercut into your opponent's lower abdomen

C) Double Penetrating Uppercut - With both fists, the right longer than the left, uppercut into your opponent's lower abdomen

3    4

D) Hook, uppercut - Hook with your left palm bringing it to your left ribs as you uppercut with your right fist aimed at the lower abdomen. Twist into a right bow stance as you uppercut.

E) Double Closing Scissor - Close your right hand and left hand together, the left fist near your right elbow, closing them infront of your centerline thereby making a scissor action, to break your opponent's left arm.

5

## （五）下盤屈馬

① 雙搶—屈馬雙掌推搶敵人下盤馬步。
② 開弓彈—屈馬用右掌開弓彈削擊敵人膝蓋。
③ 屈馬揽—屈馬用揽手搶敵人左拳。
④ 屈馬開—屈馬右手掌開敵人。
⑤ 屈馬雙搏—屈馬雙搏解敵人屈馬雙搶。

## 5. LOWER POSITION KNEELING STANCE TECHNIQUE

1) Double Palm Strike — Crouch into a kneeling stance and strike out with both palms

2) Open Bow Snapping Chop - Crouch into a kneeling stance and snap your right palm into a side chop

3) Kneeling Grab — Crouch into a kneeling stance as you grab with your right and left hand

4) **Kneeling Openhand Block** – Crouch into a kneeling stance; slice your right hand down to your right side, performing a right open hand block.
5) **Kneeling Double Splitting Block** - Crouch into a kneeling stance and spread your right and left hands outward to block.

I-1　　　　I-2

## 五祖拳之腿法

### （一）　　踩　　腿

① 甲方用右拳直撞乙方心胸部，乙方右手開出用踩腿踩踏甲方右腿面骨　② 。

## LEG TECHNIQUES OF THE NGO CHO KUN

1) Cutting Kick

1. A attacks by punching into B's chest; B blocks the punch with his right arm and delivers a right cutting kick into A's sheen bone (2)

II-1　　　　II-2

I-3.　　　　　　　　　　　　　　　　　　　　　　　　II-4

## （二）　　掃　割　手

① 掃割手　　　第一勢動式
② 掃割手　　　第二勢定式：用右脚掃並用右手掌掃割敵人腰側。

II-5　　II-6

39

用　　法

③ 甲乙雙方子午中肢對接。
④ 乙方先攻左手拳開脫。
⑤ 乙方直進右足右手拳撞擊甲方面部，甲方走馬閃左畔。
⑥ 甲方同時並用右脚掃乙方右脚，右手掌掃劏乙方右腰側使乙方撲倒。

2) Cutting Hand Sweep

1. Cock your right arm towards your left in preparation for a side chop

2. Putting your weight on the left legs, sweep forward with your right leg as you chop with your right palm

APPLICATIONS:

3. A and B both assume the center arm classical engrande stance

4. B attacks by first opening A's arm by a downward block

5. B immediately steps in with his right leg and delivers a right punch to A's face; A evades the punch by moving sideways ready to

6. Counter with a cutting hand sweep to knock down B.

III-1    III-2

（三） 連環掃割手，掃內割手
① 掃割手　　第一勢動式
② 掃割手　　第二勢定式

3) Continuous Cutting Hand Sweep

1. Cock your right arm towards your left

2. Sweep forward with your right leg and chop with your right palm

III-3   III-4

③ 掃內割　　第一勢動式
④ 掃內割　　第二勢定式

3. Shift your weight to your left leg as you retract your right arm ready for a tiger claw, and block upward with your left hand

4. Continue by sweeping your right foot backwards into a bow stance position, and strike with a right tiger claw.

III-5

用　　法

⑤　甲乙雙方白馬卸蹄式。
⑥　甲方先攻路右足右手拳撞，乙方用右手挑。
⑦　乙方順勢用右脚掃甲方右脚，並用右手掌掃甲方右腰側。
⑧　甲方閃馬以右拳鞭擊乙方面部，乙方左手挑。
⑨　乙方右脚掃內割，並用右手虎爪掌推擋甲方前胸。

APPLICATIONS

5. A and B both assume the horse stance

6. A step forward with his right leg and attacks B with a right punch; B blocks the punch with his right hand.

7. B proceeds countering with a right cutting hand sweep; A evades the cutting hand sweep by lifting his right leg and moving sideways to evade the chop.

8. A steps down his right foot and counters with a right whip (backfist) punch to B's head; B blocks the whip punch with his left hand.

9. After blocking, B immediately sweeps backward with his right leg and simultaneously hit A's chest with a right tiger claw to knock down A.

III-6

III-7

III-8

III-9

IV-1

## （四） 盤剪法

① 盤剪法　　　第一勢：右手掌開，右腿屈馬成左穿搜步。

4) Scissor Kick

1. Crouch down with your left leg and block with your right hand.

IV-3

② 盤剪法　　第二勢：用腰力轉向右畔，全身離地，盤左足力掃剪。
③ 盤剪法　　第三勢

2. Using the force of your left leg, spring upwards towards your right lifting your whole body in mid-air.

3. Land on your right side as your left leg swing towards your right completing the scissor kick.

IV-2

IV-4

用　　法
④ 甲乙雙方相對峙
⑤ 甲方起右脚踢乙方，乙方側閃左畔左穿梭步　第一勢
⑥ 乙方盤左剪勁勢　第一式
⑦ 乙方盤剪左脚掃剪倒甲方　第二式


APPLICATIONS

4. A & B stand on guard

5. A attacks with a right front kick; B evades the kick by moving towards his right, crouching down ready to counter with the scissor kick.

6. Immediately upon evading, B leaps forward with his left leg, sliding his right leg inside A's left leg.

7. B completes the scissor kick by swinging his left leg into A's leg

IV-5

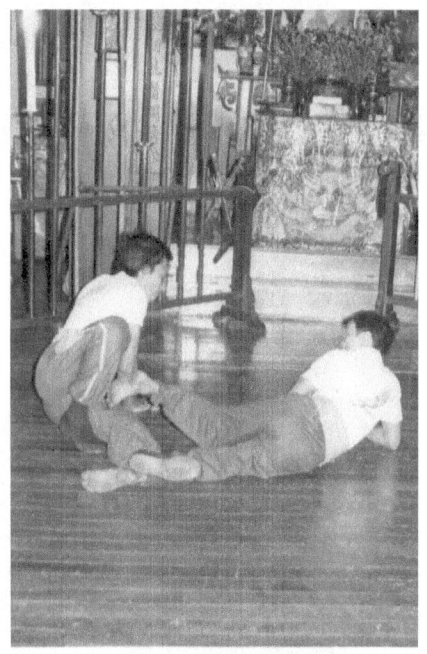

IV-6     IV-7

# 五祖拳肢手用法

「五祖門下要切磋武功或較量肢手搏擊橋手皆用此子午中肢一招。」
陳少堂　　郭德利

## PRACTICAL APPLICATIONS OF NGO CHO KUN TECHNIQUES

1. The "Chi-Ngo Tiong Ki" (center arm position) classical on-guard position of Ngo Cho Kun is used whenever a Ngo Cho Kun stylist wants to test, contest or fight with an adversary. To the Ngo Cho stylist, this technique symbolizes Ngo Cho kung fu, so that if they meet and opponent with the same stance, immediately, they could identify each other as brothers and then dispute could be settled amicably.

11-1

I-2

（一）　　　雙 批 手

① 甲方右拳鞭乙方面部，乙方右手掀。
② 甲方雙批右擊乙方右腰側並用右腳掃乙方右脚。

Techniques:

I Double Chop

1. A attacks with a right whip punch (backfist) to B's face; B blocks with his right arm.

2. A immediately steps in with his right foot to sweep B's right foot and double chop with his right and left palm into B's side of the waist.

II-1    II-2

## （二）　　雙竪拳

① 甲方白馬卸蹄，乙方子午中肢。
② 甲方踏右足右拳撞乙方胸部，乙方踏右足右手拳開。

**II Double Straight Punch**

1. A stands in the white horse position; B is in the classical center arm position

2. A step forward with his right foot and punches B's chest; B blocks the punch with his right hand

II-3　II-4

③ 乙方脫手。
④ 並用雙豎拳直擊甲方心胸。

3. B immediately follows the block with another left arm block to open A's right arm

4. and follows up with a double straight punch into A's heart

   Note: 2,3,4 should be performed in a continuous motion as one technique.

1

（三）　　　孩兒抱牌，虎爪掌

① 甲乙雙方子午中肢雙接。

III Child Holding the Tablet Palm, Tiger Claw

1. A and B are both in the Ngo Cho classical center arm position as their arm connect

III-2　　　　　　　　　　III-3

② 甲方先下手爲強，左手脫並用孩兒抱牌式直撞擊乙方。
③ ④ 乙方走馬閃左畔右掌開，同時移形扱位走馬閃在甲方背後。
⑤ 用虎爪掌擋擊甲方後背心。

2. B takes the move by opening up A's arm with his left arm and attacks with a "child holding the tablet palm strike (3)

4. B immediately counters by moving sideways evading the palm strike and blocking out with the right open hand

5. B continues the evasion by stepping into the back of A, and strikes A at the back with a powerful right tiger claw.

    NOTE : This is a highly advanced Ngo Cho technique, whereby the defender evades the opponent's attack by moving to his back and then countering.

III-4

III-5

V.1

（四）　　　青龍點，雙掛手，獅子翻身

① 甲乙雙方皆白馬卸蹄式。

IV Green Dragon Spot, Double Palm Strike, "Lion Body Turning Scissor Kick".

A. A and B assume the white horse position.

IV-2, IV-3

② 甲方踏右足青龍點攻乙方左太陽穴，乙方退右足，左手挑。
③ 甲方踏左足，左青龍點攻乙方右太陽穴，乙方退左足，右手挑。

2. A steps forward with his right foot, strikes a "green dragon spot (roundhouse punch) into B's left temple; B steps backward with his right foot and blocks his left hand

3. A steps forward with his left foot, strikes a "green dragon spot" (left roundhouse punch) into B's right temple; B steps backward with his left foot and blocks with his right hand.

IV-4

IV-5

④ 甲方踏右足，雙掛手直擋擊乙方胸部，動式　第一勢
⑤　　　　　　　　　　　　　　　　　　　　第二勢
⑥ 乙方順勢借力倒向天獅式。
⑦⑧ 再用獅仔翻身式右足盃掃剪甲方右脚使甲方撲倒。

IV-6

IV-7

4 & 5. A continues the attack by stepping forward with his right foot and hitting B's chest with a double palm strike

6. B "drifts" along with the force of A's double palm strike by slipping down into the "lion body turning" position.

7 & 8. Using the lion body turning position, B delivers a scissor kick into A's right foot, making A fall down

IV-8

NOTE : This is a highly advanced technique, perfect timing is needed in executing the scissor kick.

四門刈團體操

雙緩拳團體操

# CHAPTER VII - COMPLETE LIST OF NGO CHO KUN·TO ·FORM

雙捎拳團體操　Group practice of Sang Sou Kun Double Round House

# 第七章 五祖拳法全部拳套
## 陳少堂

自達摩開元。太祖始教。繼而羅漢白鶴行者等。接踵而起。或專內家。或練外家。剛柔各有所長。法門變化多端。但萬花開一樹。千拳歸一法。至清末一代。蔡玉鳴師祖。集一身所學。溶太祖羅漢白鶴達尊齊天各派於一爐。取長棄短。而成為白鶴指。齊天掌。太祖足。羅漢步。達尊身創立五祖門拳法。別開生面。自成一家。其拳路剛柔相濟。寓剛於柔。不論男婦老幼。如經常鍛練五祖拳法。可以促進人體新陳代榭。改善與提高內臟氣官功能。增強體質。此外還可以提高禦敵。攻防。培養靈敏果敢之優良品質。

五祖拳主要內容。有徒手和器械二種。徒手套拳共有四十四套。器械方面有關刀。方天戟。梅花左槍。長短棍法。扁担。斬馬刀。單刀。雙劍雙鞭。雙拐。等。徒手拳套四十四套中。有多套可二人對抖。（頂技套拳不算在內）。

**THE COMPLETE LIST OF NGO-CHO KUN TO (FORMS)**

Since the beginning of Tamo, there has been numerous teachings on the different styles and philosophies of kung-fu. Among these are the Lo han, the White Crane and the Monkey, and many others, both internal and external styles. Though the different styles may vary, they trace their origins to only one root: the Shaolin. During the declining years of the Ching Dynasty, Sijo Chua Giok Beng combined and grouped together the salient features of Tai-Cho, Lo-Han, White Crane, Monkey Tamo: the finger strikes of White Crane, the palm techniques of the Monkey, the kicking of Tai-Cho, the stepping of the Lo-Han, the posture of Tamo. These excellent features he consolidated in forming the Ngo Cho Kun Wat (The Way of the Five Ancestral Fist), making it a distinct style, a beautiful blend of both the hard and soft styles, a style highly recommended to students of all ages. Diligent practice of the Ngo Cho Kun can balance the metabolism, strengthen the internal organs, improve one's general health being. Aside from this, Ngo Cho is a very effective from of self-defense.

The Ngo Cho Kun is made up of fist forms and weaponry. There are 44 different kun-to (fist forms). On weaponry, there is the kwan knife, the long speark hook, skip halberd, plum flower left hand spear, long and short staff, pin-ta peddler's pole, single saber, horse cutting knife, double sword, double short-whip (sai), double clutches (tonfa). Most of the 44 fist forms could be practised with a partner like the pre-arranged sparring. This pre-arranged sparring is called ting ki which is a different study from that of the fist forms.

Sigung Tan Kiong Beng was one of the Sijo's most trusted students, and being with the sijo for a long time, he was able to learn the complete form of Ngo Cho kun.

師祖衣砵弟子陳京銘師公。追隨師祖最久。得傳授全部拳套及器械法。茲將全部拳套名稱列下。

- (一) 五祖拳立法三　戰
- (二) 五祖拳立法三才戰　又名天地人戰
- (三) 平馬戰
- (四) 鳳尾戰
- (九) 五虎戰
- (十) 瑞華戰
- (土) 二十拳
- (圭) 雙摏拳
- (宝) 四門打角
- (齿) 四門挑截
- (甴) 走馬四門拳
- (圡) 十字拳
- (甶) 六合拳
- (甹) 茵篷踢
- (甼) 兩儀 即二節
- (四一) 雙鞭法
- (四二) 回馬搖
- (四三) 連環八卦
- (四四) 雙龍抱印
- (四五) 獅仔翻身
- (四六) 孩兒抱
- (五四) 七十二勢地煞法

- (四) 左戰法
- (五) 鶴戰法
- (六) 直弓戰
- (七) 龍頭戰
- (古) 雙綏拳
- (宝) 三戰十字
- (共) 四門割
- (圥) 千字打
- (夭) 對粧即追蹤拳
- (元) 四門走底
- (卅) 三才 即三節
- (圭) 四鳳 即四節
- (圭) 三角搖
- (卅) 三肶胅頭
- (卅) 五肶胅頭
- (卅) 中綰法
- (卅) 飛鶴雙爪法
- (卅) 鼓推鞭
- (卅) 白猿出洞
- (五一) 清風法
- (五二) 連城法
- (五三) 三十六勢天罡法

六門手法及八法手。乃較技撲擊手法。爲師祖之絕技。故當師祖生前所設仁義堂武館。大門外有楹聯一對。上聯是手執八法稱無敵。下聯是足踏蓮花第一人。

# THE COMPLETE LIST OF NGO CHO KUN TO (FIST FORMS)
## By Benito Tan

1. NGO CHO LIP WAT SAM CHIEN (The Foundation of Ngo Cho Sam Chien)
2. NGO CHO LIP WAT SAM CHAYCHIEN (The Foundation of Ngo Cho Sam Chay Chien - also known as Tian Te Lin Chian)
3. PIENG MA CHIEN (Even Stance Chien)
4. CHO CHIEN WAT (Left Chien)
5. HO CHIEN WAT (Crane's Chien)
6. TIT KIENG CHIEN (Straight Bow Chien)
7. LIENG TAO CHIEN (Dragon's Head Chien)
8. HONG BE CHIEN (Phoenix Tail Chien)
9. NGO HO CHIEN (Five Tiger Chien)
10. SUI HWA CHIEN
11. LI SIP KUN (Twenty Punch)
12. SANG SOU KUN (Double Roundhouse Punch)
13. SE MUN PA KAK (Hitting the Four Coeners)
14. SONG SUI KUN
15. SAM CHIEN SIP LI
16. SE MUN KWA (Four Direction Sweep)
17. CHIAN LI TA (Chopping Attack)
18. TUI CHONG (Pursuing Fist)
19. SE MUN CHO TUE (Attacking the Lower Four Directions)
20. SE MUN TIAO CHA (Deflecting/Intercepting the Four Directions)
21. CHO BE SE MUN KUN (Walking the Four Direction Fist)
22. SIP LI KUN (Cross Punch)
23. LAK HAP KUN (Six Harmonious Fists)
24. IN TIT TAT (Enthwining Kick)
25. LIONG GI (Two Segments)
26. SAM CHAY (Third Segments)
27. SE HONG (Fourth Segment)
28. SA KAK YIAO (Three Corners Rocking Punch)
29. SAM TO TIN TO (Three Times Hitting the Head)
30. NGO TO TIM TAO (Five Times Hitting the Head)
31. TIONG KWAN WAT
32. SANG PIAN WAT (Double Whip Strike)
33. WEY MA YIAO (Turning Stance Rocking Punch)
34. LIAN KWAN PAKUA (Linking Pakua)
35. SANG LIENG PO IN (Double Dragon Fist)
36. SAI TZE WAN SIN (Lion Body Turning Fist)
37. HI LI PO ("Child Holding the Tablet" Fist)
38. HUI HO SANG LIAO (Double Claw of the Flying Crane)
39. KO TWI PI
40. PE GUAN CHU TONG (White Ape Exit From the Cave)
41. CHIENG HONG WAT
43. SACHAP LAK TIAN KONG WAT (36 Steps of the Monkey)
44. CHI CHAP LI TUE SWAT WAT (72 Steps Comet Fist)

LAK MUN CHIU WAT (6 Direction Hands) and PAT WAT (8-Method Hands) are the deadly secret techniques of the founder Sijo Chua Giok Beng. In hi lifetime, he hanged couplet tablet at the entrance of his Lin Tek Tong gym nasium which read symbolically:

" THE HANDS WITH THE PAT WAT (8 Methods) is unbeatable; The Fee Stepping on the Lotus, I'm Number One."

## 五祖拳開始法五式

凡五祖拳門下起拳皆用此五式：
第一式　鐵鎚沉江
　　雙脚坐平馬，雙手握拳由下用力抽至兩脅下第一勢，第二勢，二勢合式。

### QI KUN (The Opening Fist)

The five techniques of the Opening Fist serves as the bow of the NGO CHO Kun and is used in every kun-to (fist forms) of the NGO CHO kun. These five techniques symbolizes the NGO CHO kun.

TECHNIQUE NUMBER 1 :　TI TUI TING KANG ("Metal Hammer Sinking Into the River")

Pic. 1 & 2: Standing in the horse stance, thrust clenched fists forward and using strength, slowly pull your hands up to the sides of your ribs.

1

2

3

4

第二式　金蟬脫殼
　　雙舉雙掌由兩脅下膳落。
第三式　美女梳粧
　　雙手由下方交叉轉向上與眉齊平。

TECHNIQUE NUMBER 2 :　KIM CHIAN TUAT KOCK ("Golden Cicada Shedding Off Its Skin)

Open fists as you thrust downward with the palms facing the floor (Pic. 3). Fingers should face towards each other.

TECHNIQUE NUMBER 3 :　BI LIN SUE CHENG ("The Lady Fixing Her Make-up")

Swing both hands upwards with the two hands crisscrossing infront of your body and spread them outwards into eyebrow level bending and tucking in the elbow with the fingers of both hands pointing outward (Pic. 4)

5　　　　　　　　　　　　　　　6

第四式　關平抱印
右拳左掌推至對心胸，即五湖四海皆兄弟行禮式，二勢合一式。

TECHNIQUE NUMBER 4 :　KWAN PENG PO IN ("Gen. Kwan Peng Holding the Seal)

From Technique Number 3, pull your right fist back to your right side at the ribs and bring your left palm down towards your right fist covering it (the right fist). Pic. 5

Slowly stretch your right fist and left palm together outward infront of your chest forming the traditional kung fu bow, which means everywhere all men are brothers (Pic. 6).

7          8

第五式　雙龍搶珠
　　右拳變掌由兩骨下駿肼吐出第一勢動式，第二勢定式。
　　每套五祖拳起拳皆用此五式。

TECHNIQUE NUMBER 5 :　　SANG LIENG CHIU TSU ("Double Dragon Fighting for the Pearl)

Release the hold (or contact) of both hands and with palms facing upward slowly bring both palms at their respective sides, i. e., to the sides of the ribs (Pic. 7).
As you bring your palms to your sides, slowly twist your torso to one side, the right side. The tips of the fingers should be at nipple level. As you bring the palms forward, use tension and twist the upper torso to the proper front position. Bring both palms forward with the palms facing outward, fingers pointing upward. (pic. 8)

1

2

五祖拳收拳式　　　SIU KUN (Closing Fist)
每套五祖拳收拳皆用此二式

Every NGO CHO kun to (form) is finished by closing with either of these two closing fists.

CLOSING TECHNIQUE NUMBER 1 : PO PAI CHIU (The Shield Holding Hand)
第一式抱牌手收拳

Stand in a right hanging stance, puch your right inverted palm slowly

Stand in a right hanging stance, puch your right inverted palm slowly out until they are infront of you. The position of both hands should be parallel to the center.

CLOSING TECHNIQUE NUMBER 2 : CHIAO YONG CHIU
第二式招揚手

Stand in a hanging stance. Close palms in a clenched fist at ear level, bring both hands at the center, with right palm at nose level, the left palm closely behind it.

Any of the above closing techniques completes the Siu Kun movement of the NGO CHO Kun.

**五祖立法　三戰　郭德利演式**

三戰為五祖拳立法基本功夫。初入門者即開始練習三戰，其法雖簡然五祖拳之基礎全在此套，至少須訓練六個月至八個月才能運用五肢力而使內勁貫通全身腰馬穩固靈活然後開始訓練其他拳套。

## SAM CHIEN

The SAM CHIEN is the basic foundation of the Ngo Cho Kun. Its movements may appear simple but don't be misled. In the SAM CHIEN are the movements which serve as the fundamental or basis of the Ngo Cho kun. Drilling exercises on the basic kun to (forms) require at least 8 months to perfect. The development of the Ngo Ki Lat (5 parts power) should be cultivated to its full extent and the ching (intrinsic energy) perfectly circulated. Similarly, the stance should be developed to afford the practitioner stability to the ground, at the same time maintaining the agility/sensitivity of the stance to respond to an attack or assault. After the student has achieved this level of power and ching development, he is now ready to advance to other kun-to (forms)

雙捎拳團體操

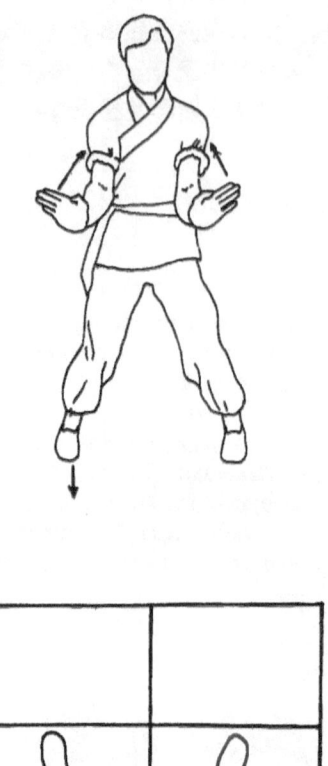

1

第一式　由五祖拳開始法第五式雙龍搶珠式起手，踏右足戰馬不丁不八，前四俊六卽前脚四分力俊脚六分力。

Begin by doing the Five Techniques of the opening fist:

Pic. 1 : From the opening fist, the 5th technique "double dragon fighting for the pearl".

第二式　雙手抽至兩脅下掌心相對。

Pic. 2 : Step forward with your right leg into a right chian be stance. In the chian be stance, the weight is distributed thus: 60% on the back leg; 40% on the front leg. Pull in both your arms until the two palms are at the sides of your ribs. Inhale through your nose as you pull back.

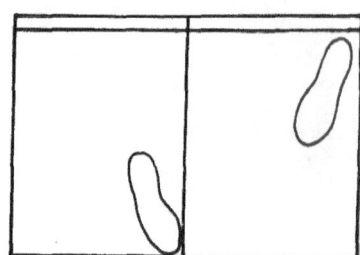

第三式　雙手發力向前直插微斜低。

Pic. 3 : Thrust out both hands, slightly slanting down, focusing your strength on your fingertips and let out a short exhalation through your mouth as you thrust out. The whole body should be tensed.

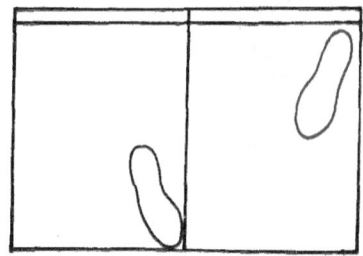

第四式　然後慢慢雙手吞肩坐節。

Pic. 4 ; Slowly bend your elbow, and stretch your finger upward facing the ceiling and suck in your shoulder, continue exhaling through your mouth. Maintain the tension within the whole body including the muscles of the neck.

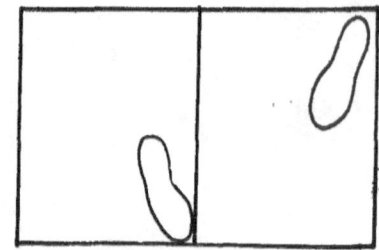

第五式 雙手掌心反轉向天。

Pic. 5 : Slowly turn your palm clockwise so that you end up with both palms facing upward.

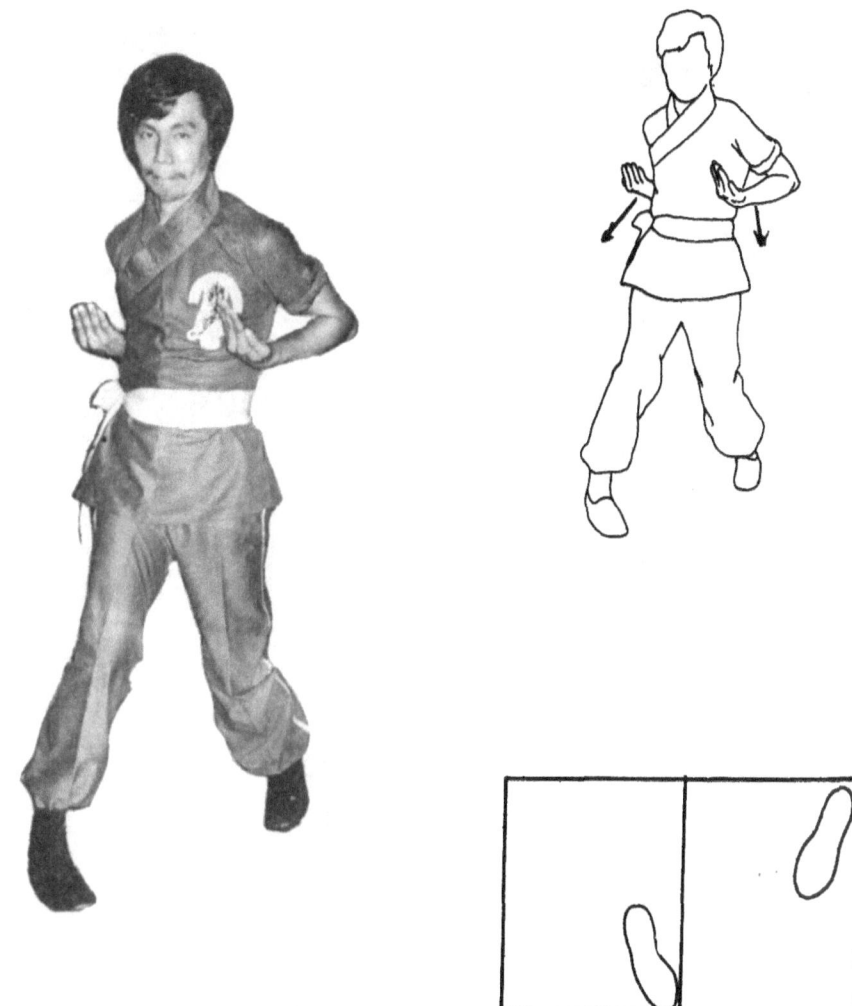

第六式　雙吞手入至兩脅下。

Pic. 6 : Simultaneously pull in/tense both arms with the palms facing upward. Slowly pull in until they reach your ribs. Inhale again through the nose. Slant sideways a little for ease.

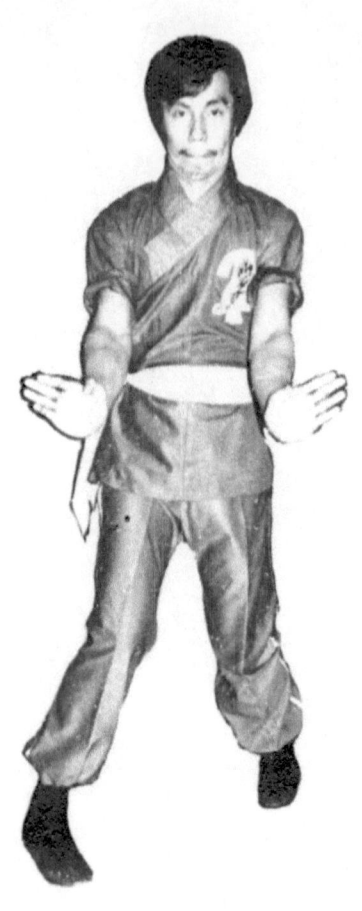

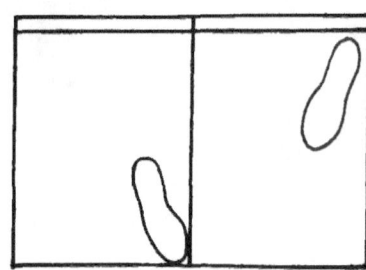

7

第七式 駿肝吐出。

Pic. 7 : Focus strength on your arms and tense your stomach as you push your arm outward in front of your stomach; exhale through your mouth as you push your hands out. Exert strength as you push your arms outward until you feel the vibration. While doing this drill, simultaneously slant your body to original position before Pic. 6.

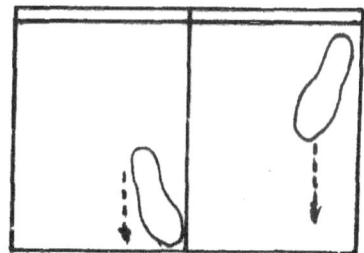

第八式 踏右足直進馬五六寸 左足隨之，雙手抽至兩脅下。

Pic. 8 : Step forward with your right leg around five inches forward with the left leg following to maintain the proper distance of the chian be stance. Pull in both arms to your ribs, inhale.

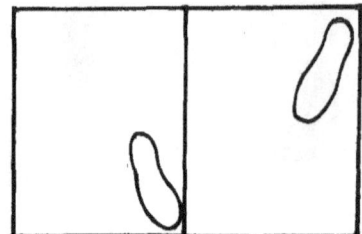

第九式　雙手發力向前直插微斜低。

Pic. 9 : Thrust out both arms, slanting downward, focus on the fingertips. Exhale shortly, abruptly.

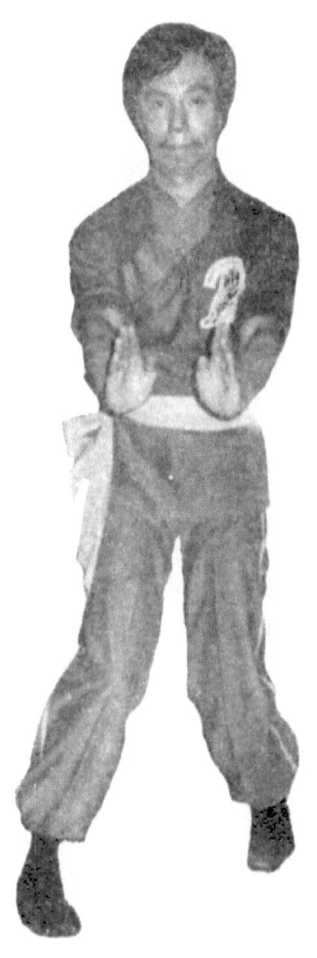

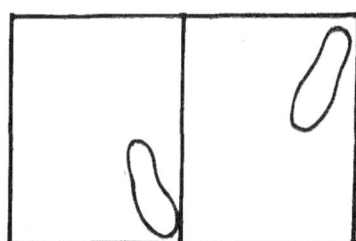

10

第十式　雙手吞肩坐節

Pic. 10 : Slowly bend your elbows as your fingers stretch upward, and such in your shoulder. Exhale.

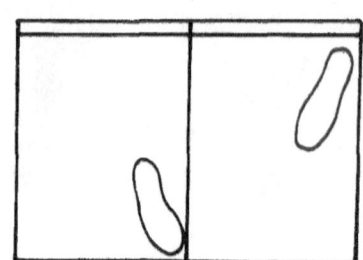

11

第十一式 雙手掌心反轉向天。

Pic. 11: Turn your palms slowly clockwise till your palms are facing upward.

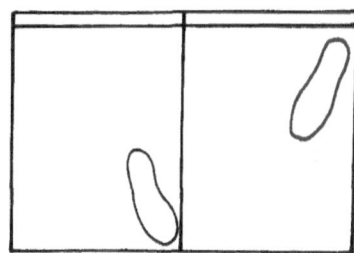

第十二式 雙吞手入至兩脅下。

Pic. 12 : Pull in both arms with tension, with the palms facing upward. Pull in slowly till they reach your ribs. Inhale

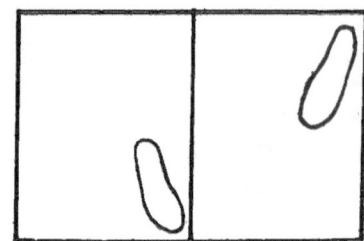

13

第十三式　駿䏢吐出。

Pic. 13 : Tense your arms and stomach till they vibrate. Push both arms forward until they are infront of your stomach. Exhale.

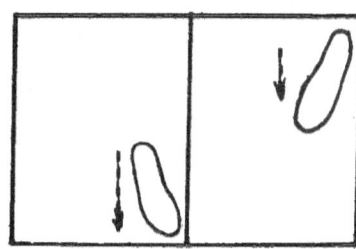

14

第十四式　踏右尾直進馬五六寸雙手抽至兩脅下。

Pic. 14 : Step forward with your right leg around five inches forward with the left leg following to maintain the proper distance the chian be stance. Pull in both arms to your ribs. Inhale.

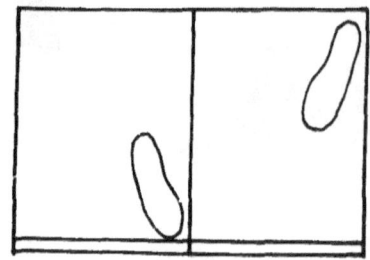

15

第十五式 雙手發力向前直插微斜低。

Pic. 15: Thrust out with both arms, slightly slanting downward, exerting strength on your thrust. Focus on the finger tips: Exhale abruptly.

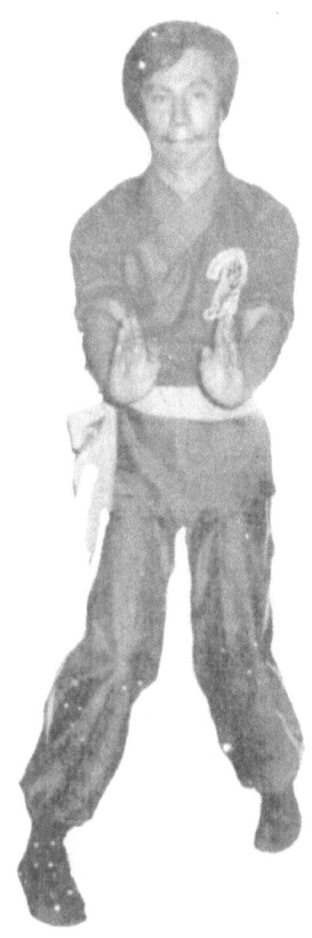

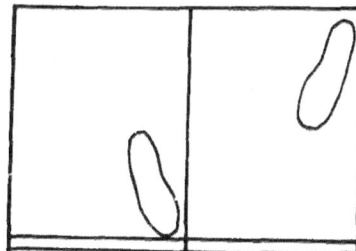

16

第十六式　雙手慢慢吞肩坐節。

Pic. 16 : Slowly bend your elbow as your fingers stretch upward. Suck in your shoulders. Exhale.

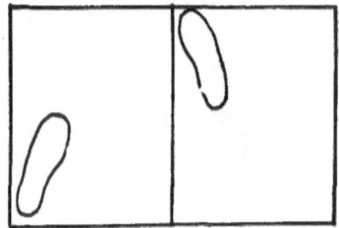

17

第十七式　雙手掌心反轉向天。

Pic. 17 :　Turn your palms slowly clockwise till they are facing upwards.

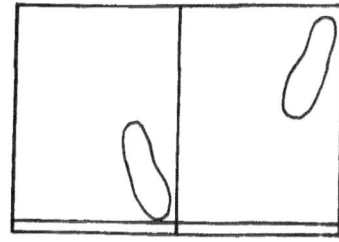

第十八式　雙吞手入至雙兩脅下。

Pic. 18 : Pull in both arms with tension till they reach your ribs. Inhale.

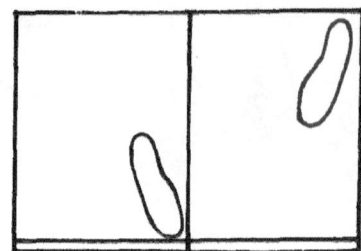

19

第十九式　駿肼吐出。

Pic. 19: Tense your arms and stomach till they vibrate and exhale as you puch your arms outward till they are infront of your stomach

NOTE: The complete movement is from Pic. 1-7. Pics. 8-19 are just repetitions of Pics. 1-7. However, this is the essence of the drills. Repetitious drilling to increase/develop strength and power.

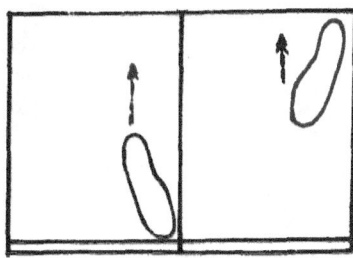

20

第二十式 退左足直退馬五六寸再直退右足雙手抽至兩脅下。

Pic. 20 : Step backwards by moving first with your left leg 5 inches backward, with the front right leg following to maintain the proper chian be stance. Pull in both arms into your ribs' side as you inhale through your nose.

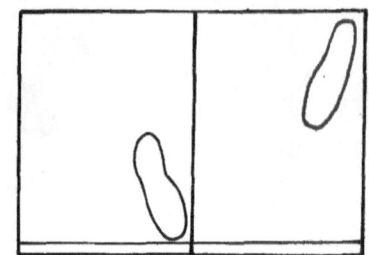

21

第二十一式　雙手發力向前直插微斜低。

Pic. 21 : Thrust out with both arms, slightly slanting downward, exerting strength on your thrust, focusing on the strength on your thrust, focusing on the strength flowing down your finger tips. Exhale briefly through the mouth.

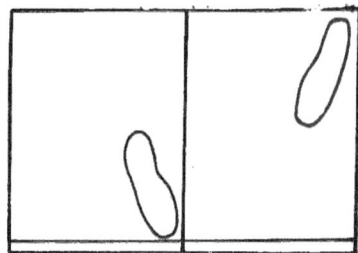

22

第二十二式　雙手慢慢吞肩坐節。

Pic. 22 : Slowly bend your elbow as your fingers stretch upward. Suck in your shoulders. Exhale through your mouth as you are bending your elbow.

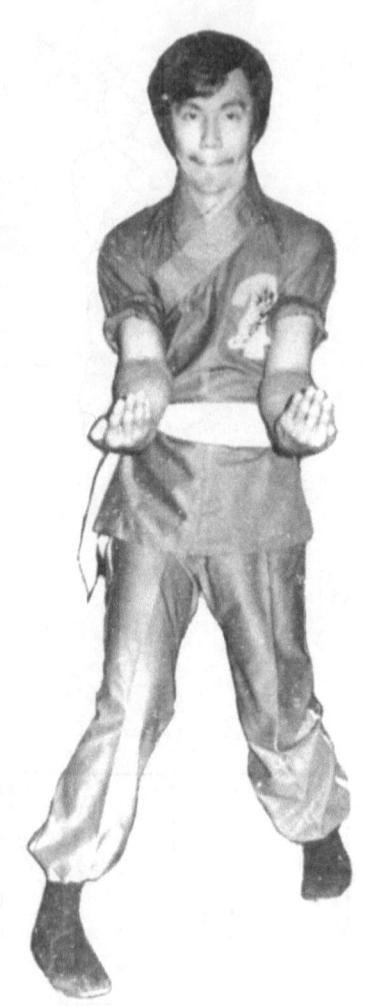

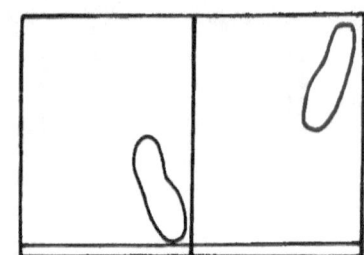

23

第二十三式　雙手掌心反轉向天。

Pic. 23 : Turn your palm slowly clockwise till they are facing upwards.

24

第二十四式　雙吞手入至兩脅下。

Pic. 24 : Tensing the arms, pull them in until they reach the ribs. Inhale through the nose as you pull in.

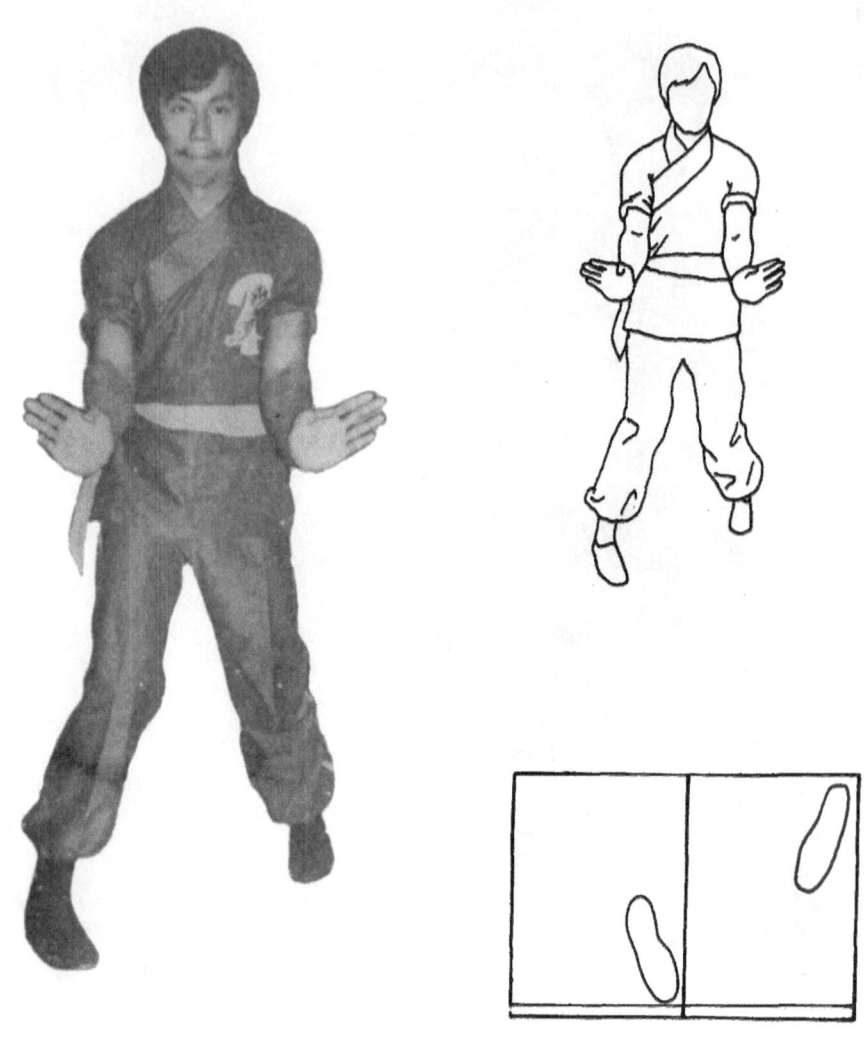

第二十五式　駿肸吐出。

Pic. 25 : Tense your arms and stomach until they vibrate. Exhale through your mouth as you push your arms outward infront of your stomach.

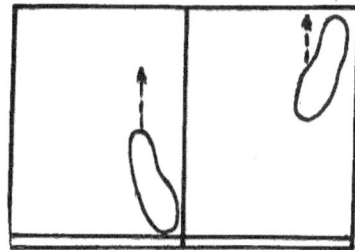

26

第二十六式　退左足直退馬五六寸**再直退右足**雙手抽至兩脅下

Pic. 26 : Step backwards by first moving your left leg 5 inches backward and the right leg following closely behind to maintain the proper distance of the chian be stance. Pull both arms until they reach your ribs. Inhale through your nose.

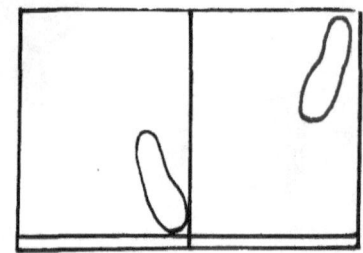

27

第二十七式　雙手發力向前直插微斜低。

Pic. 27 : Thrust out both arms, slanting slightly downward, with strength focus on the fingertips. Exhale briefly through the mouth.

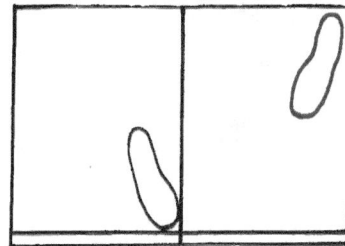

28

第二十八式　雙手慢慢吞肩坐節。

Pic. 28 : Slowly bend the elbows and stretch the fingers upward. Suck in the shoulders. Exhale.

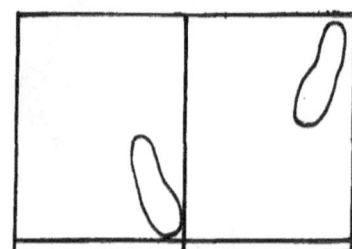

29

第二十九式　雙手掌心反轉向天。

Pic. 29 : Turn your palms slowly clockwise until they are facing upward, elbows tucked near your stomach.

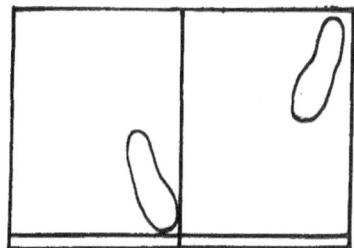

30

第三十式　雙吞手入至兩脅下。

Pic. 30 : Tensing the arms, pull them in until they reach your ribs. Inhale through the nose as you pull in slowly.

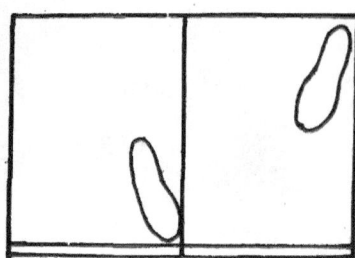

31

第三十一式　駿肝吐出。

Pic. 31 : Tense your arms and stomach until they vibrate. Exhale through your mouth as you push your arms out towards the front of your stomach.

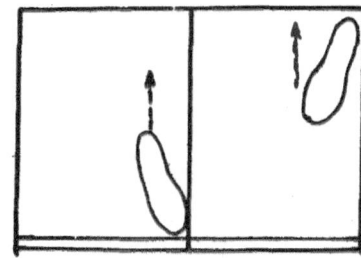

32

第三十二式 退左足直退五六寸 再直退右足 雙手抽至兩脅下。

Pic. 32 : Step back with your left leg 5 inches backward with the right leg following to maintain the proper chian be stance. Inhale through your nose as you pull in both arms to the sides of your ribs.

33

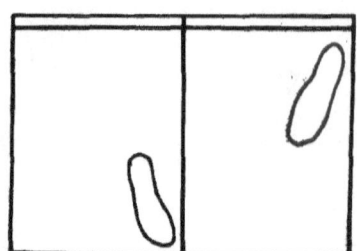

第三十三式　雙手發力向前直插微斜低。

Pic. 33 : Thrust out both arms, slightly slanting downward, exerting strength on your thrust, power focused on your finger tips. Exhale briefly through the mouth.

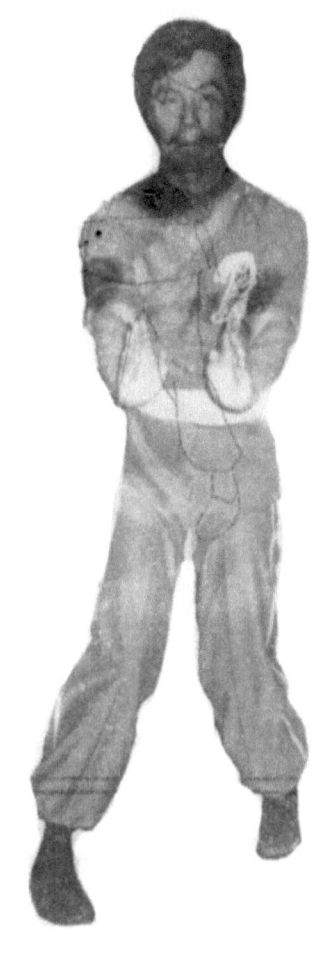

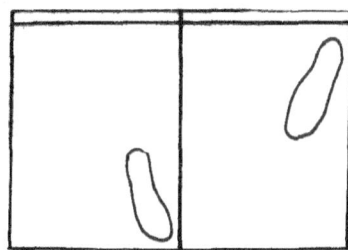

34

第三十四式　雙手慢慢吞肩坐節。

Pic. 34 : Slowly bend your elbow as your fingers stretch upward; suck in your shoulders. Exhale through your mouth,

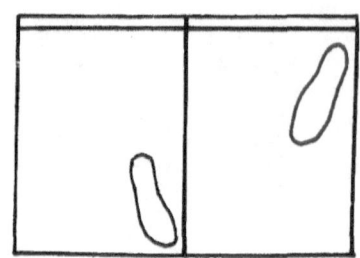

第三十五式　雙手掌心反轉向天。

Pic. 35 : Twist your palms slowly clockwise till they are facing upwards without swinging the elbow.

36

第三十六式 雙吞手入至兩脅下。

Pic. 36 : Inhale through your nose as you pull in with tension on both arms to your ribs.

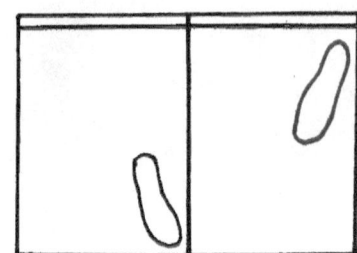

37

第三十七式　駿肼吐出。

Pic. 37 : Tensing your arms and stomach until they vibrate, exhale through the mouth as you push your palm outward infront of your stomach with the elbow bent at the sides of the stomach.

38-A

第三十八式　踏右足直進馬 左足隨之 雙關剪第一勢動式

Pic. 38A : Without moving your stance, cock in both arms with the right hand in a clenched fist, the left with open hand at the sides of your shoulders.

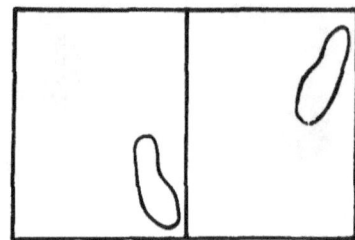

38-B

雙關剪第二勢定式

Pic. 38B : Step forward with your right leg 5 inches forward, with the left leg following behind to maintain the proper chian be stance. Close your arms, the right ahead of the left arm, infront of your nose level, completing a double closing scissor technique.

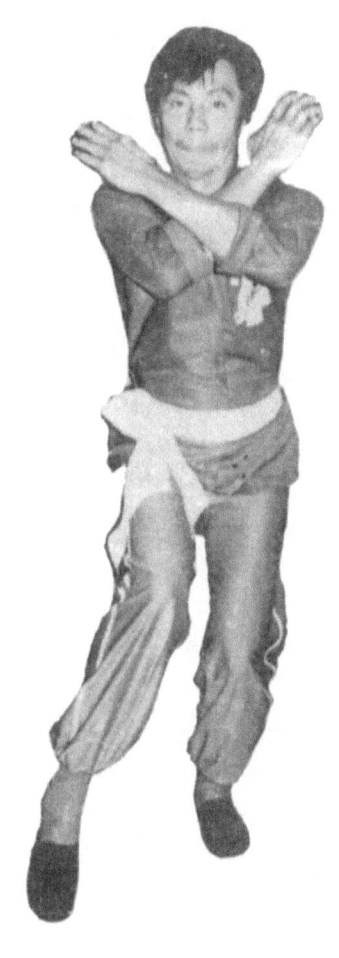

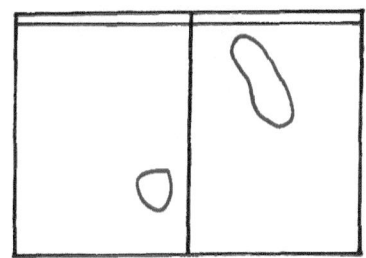

39-A

第三十九式 退左馬寄右足寄足步雙鈎手第一勢動3

Pic. 39A: Step back with your left leg into a right hanging stance and bring your arms up near your chest.

39-B

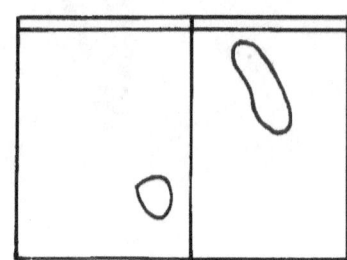

雙鉤手第二勢定式

Pic. 39B : Swing down your arms to stomach level, with elbows tucked in at the sides of your stomach, the fingers pointing down completing a double hook block.

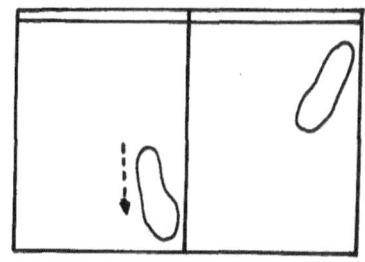

40-A

第四十式　踏進右足戰馬打節第一勢動式

Pic. 40A : Step forward with your right leg 5 inches forward and assume a right chian be stance. Pull back your right arm at the sides of your body with your fist clenched.

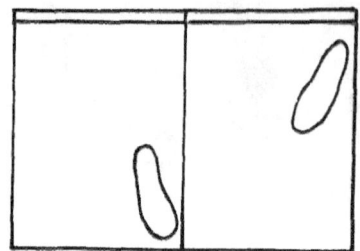

40-B

打節第二勢定式

Pic. 40B : Strike with your right elbow forward, hitting your right elbow with your left palm.

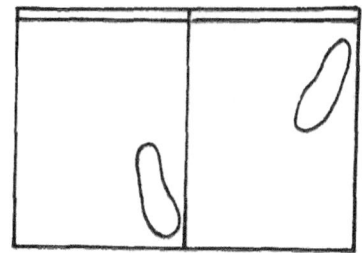

41

第四十一式　在馬右手削。

Pic. 41 : Side chop with your right palm from the elbow bend position.

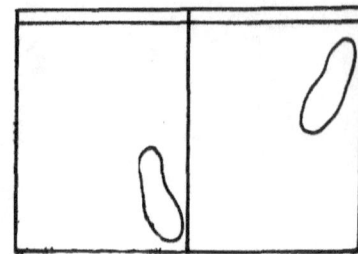

42

第四十二式　在馬左手切。

Pic. 42 : Deliver a left straight palm thrust (chiat)

43

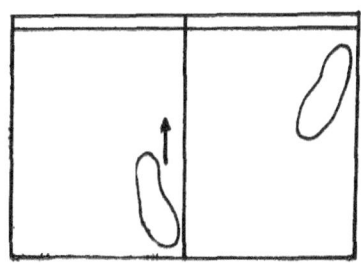

第四十三式　在馬右手釵
第四十四式　退左馬寄右足寄足步抱牌收式。

Pic. 43 : Deliver a right straight side thrust (tue). Step back with your left leg into a right hanging stance as you close with the no-pai chiu closing to finish the sam chien.

三 戰 用 法

第三十八式　用　法　　雙關剪

甲踏進左馬用左拳擊乙方喉部，乙方踏右馬用雙關剪剪斷甲方手節骨。

## APPLICATION OF SAM CHIEN

Application of the DOUBLE CLOSING SCISSOR TECHNIQUE (Pic. 38A & B)

Pic.　A punches B on the face with his left; B in a right chian be stance uses the double closing scissor technique by using his left hand to grab A's wrist and his right forearm slamming into A's elbow joint, thus breaking A's arm.

第三十九式　用　法　　寄足雙鈎手
甲踏右馬用雙撞拳擊乙方下腹丹田部，乙方退左足寄右足雙
鈎掌解甲方雙撞拳。


**Application of the DOUBLE HOOK BLOCK TECHNIQUE (Pic. 39A & B)**

Pic.　A steps in with a right chian be stance and attacks B's lower abdomen with a double uppercut; B steps back into a right hanging stance and block A's uppercut with the double hook block, B could easily counter with a right groin kick

第四十式　用　法　打節
甲踏右馬右拳揰，乙方左手擒拿並踏右馬迫身右手短節
用手肘擊甲方胸部。


Application of the Elbow Strike Side Chop, Left Straight Palm Thrust, Right Straight Side Thrust (Pic. 40 to 4B)

Pic.　A punches B with his right fist; B grabs (kim) A's right arms, his left hand and step forward pressing into A's body and counters with a right elbow strike.

第四十一，四十二，四十三式
　　用　法　　右手削，左手切，右手釵。

Pic. If A is able to evade the elbow strike by moving backwards, B continue by striking his right palm into a side chop directed into A's throat

四十一　甲方如退步閃過乙方打節，乙方急用右手削乙方喉部。
四十二　乙方再用左掌切擊甲方右腰側。
四十三　乙方同時並用右叙手擊中甲方胸部。

Pic.　B continously uses his left palm to straight thrust (chiat) into A's waist

Pic.　and finishes the attack by delivering a right straight side thrust (tui) into A's chest

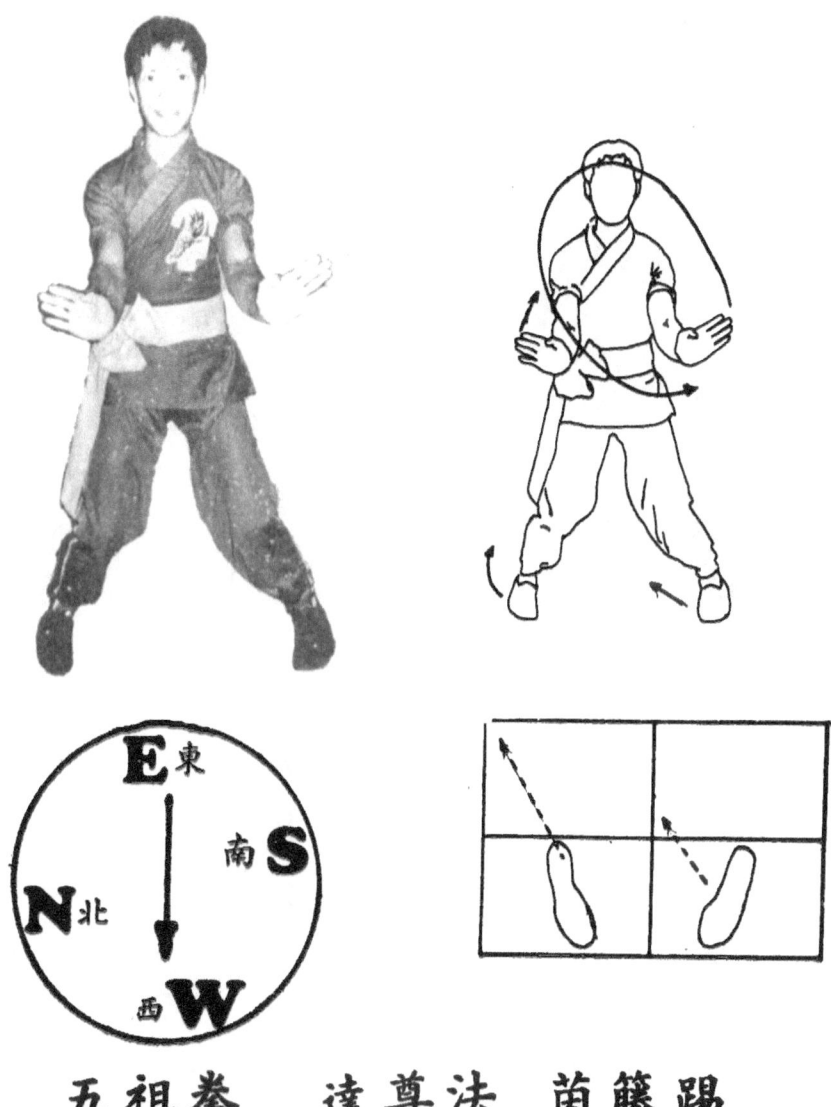

五祖拳　達尊法　茵籐踢

洪樺犀　演式

第一式：此式為五祖拳開始起拳法第五式雙龍搶珠（面向西方）。

NGO CHO KUN - Tamo's Method Enthwining Kick

Pic. 1 : Begin by performing the opening fist of Ngo Cho Kun. The picture shows the fifth technique of the opening fist "Two dragons battling for the pearl".

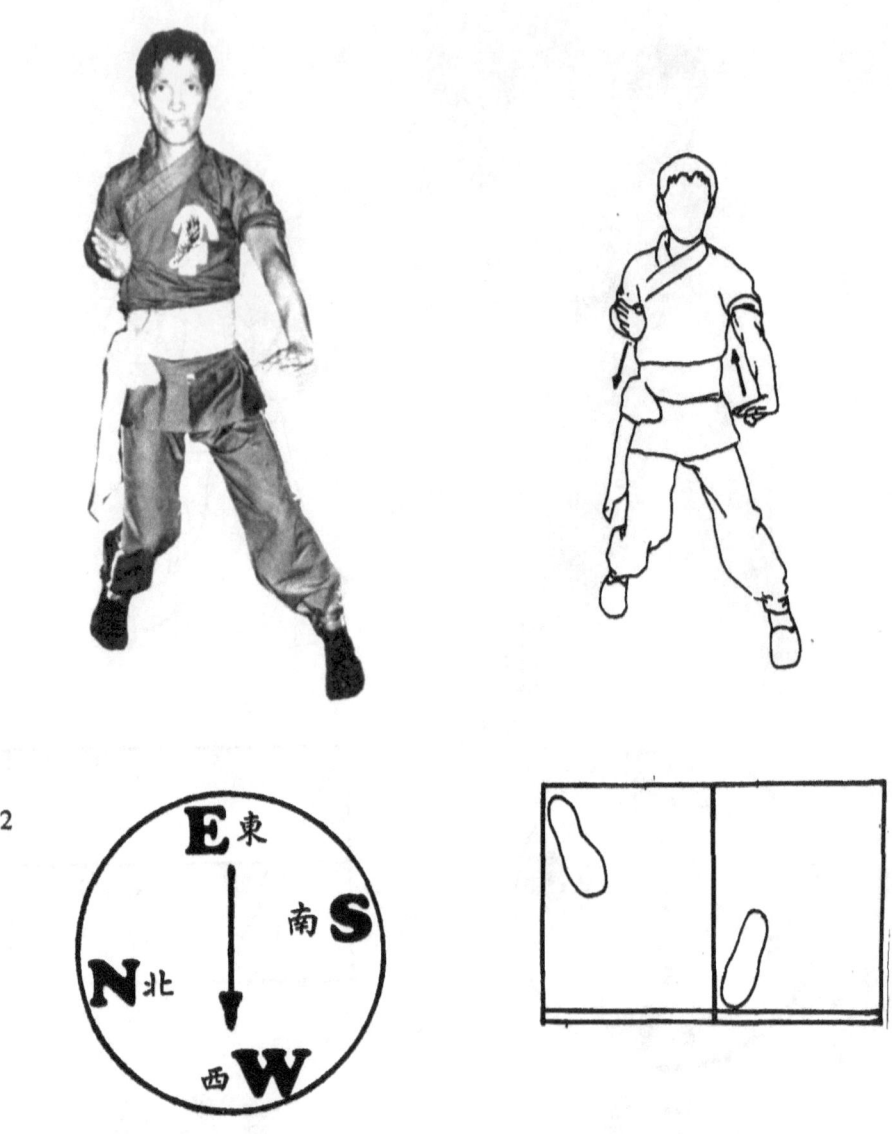

第二式：面向西方走馬閃右呷，踏左足戰馬左手掌開。

Pic. 2 : Facing your west (front), shift to your right side by stepping back with your right leg first and following with your left leg by standing in a left chian-be stance. Execute a left open hand downward block.

第三式：右手掌切。

Pic. 3 : Deliver a right slice chop

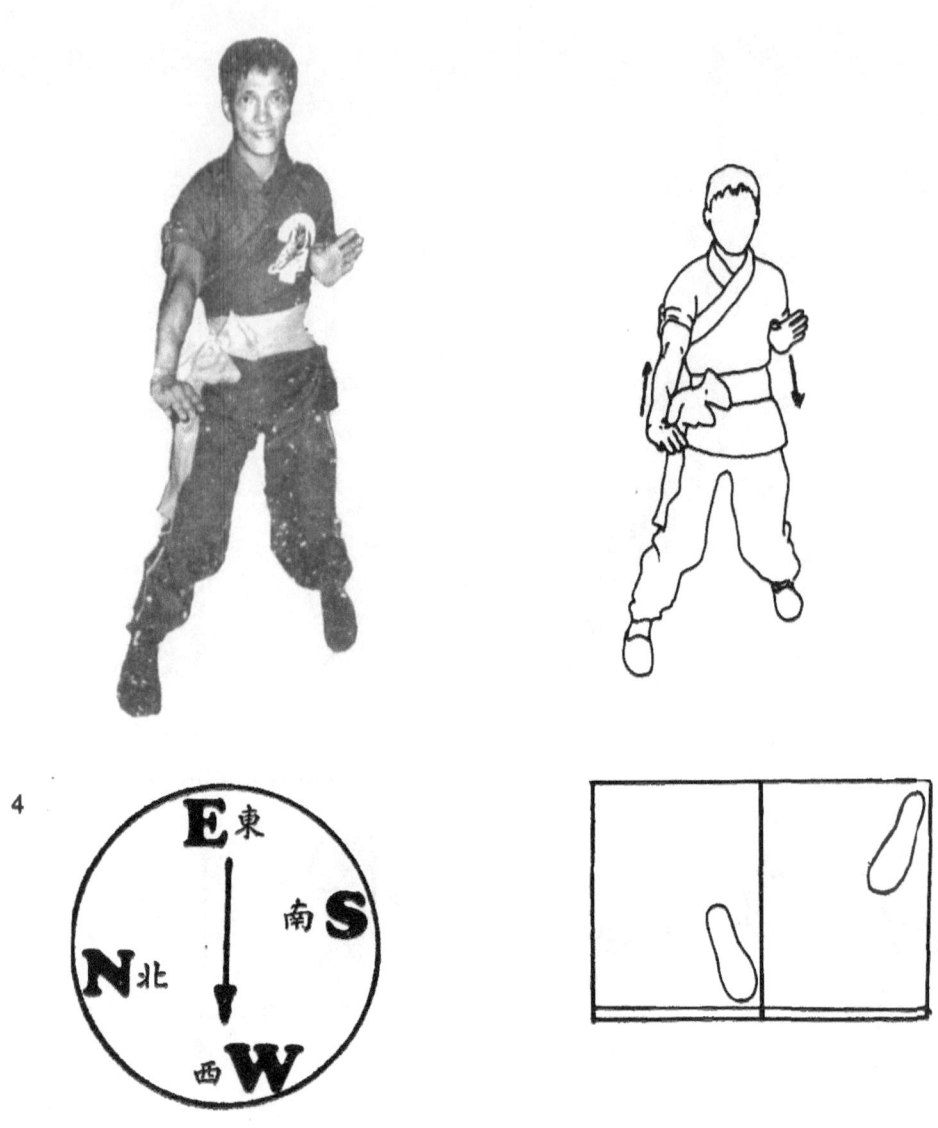

第四式：走馬閃左畔踏右足右手掌開。

Pic. 4 : Shift to your left side by stepping back with your left leg and following with your right leg into a right chian-be stance, execute a right open hand downward block.

第五式：左手掌切。

Pic. 5 : Deliver a left slice chop

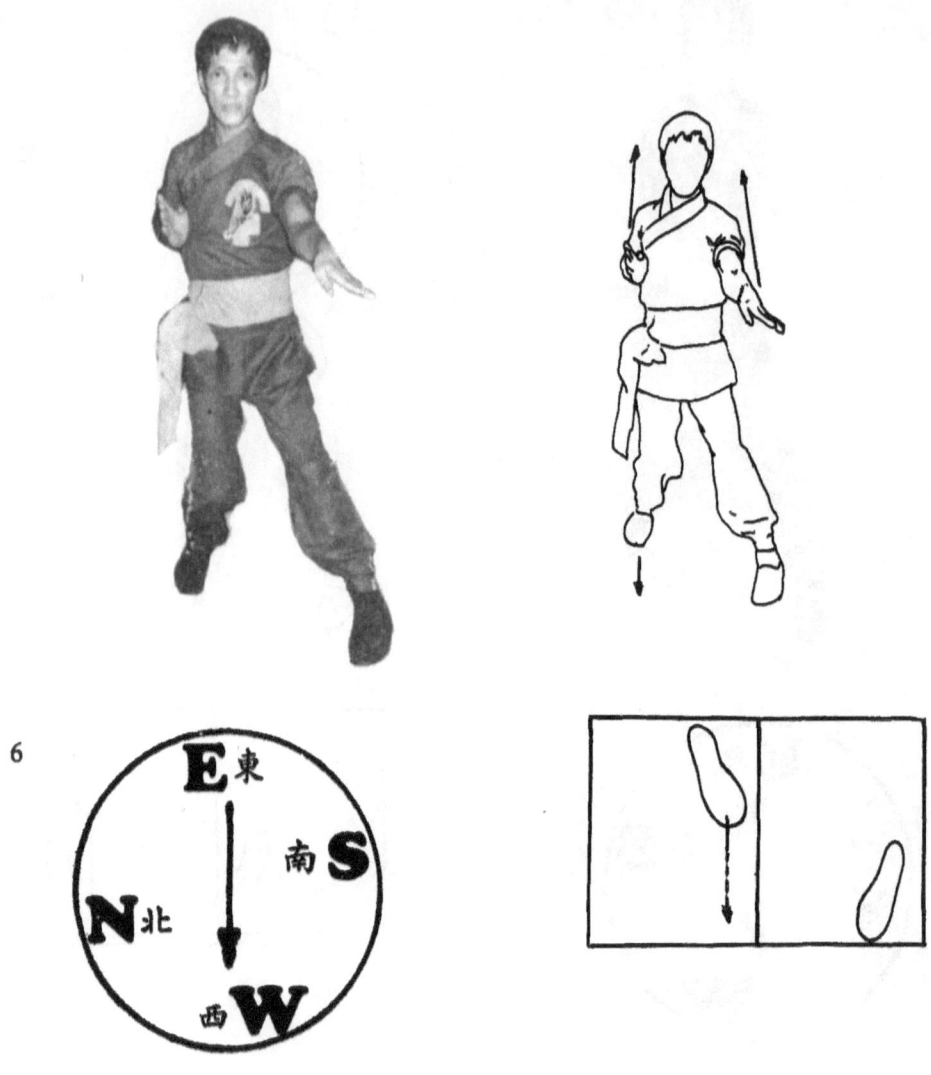

第六式：走閃中換馬踏左足左手擒。

Pic. 6 : Step forward with your right leg into a left chian be stance and execute a left grabbing block (kim).

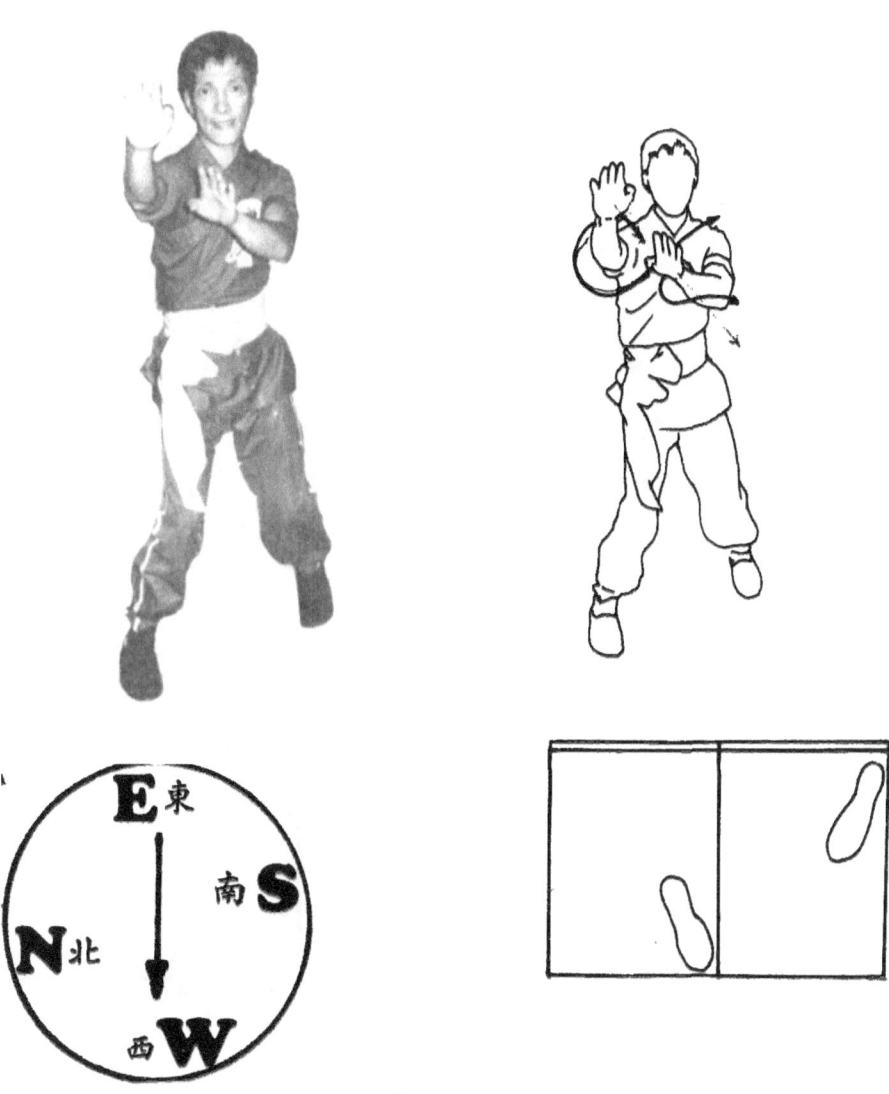

第七式：右足踏進茵簾手梭第一勢動式向西方
茵簾手梭入　　　　　第二勢合一式

Pic 7A : Step forward with your right leg into a right chian be stance; extend both hands preparing to grab your opponent's hand

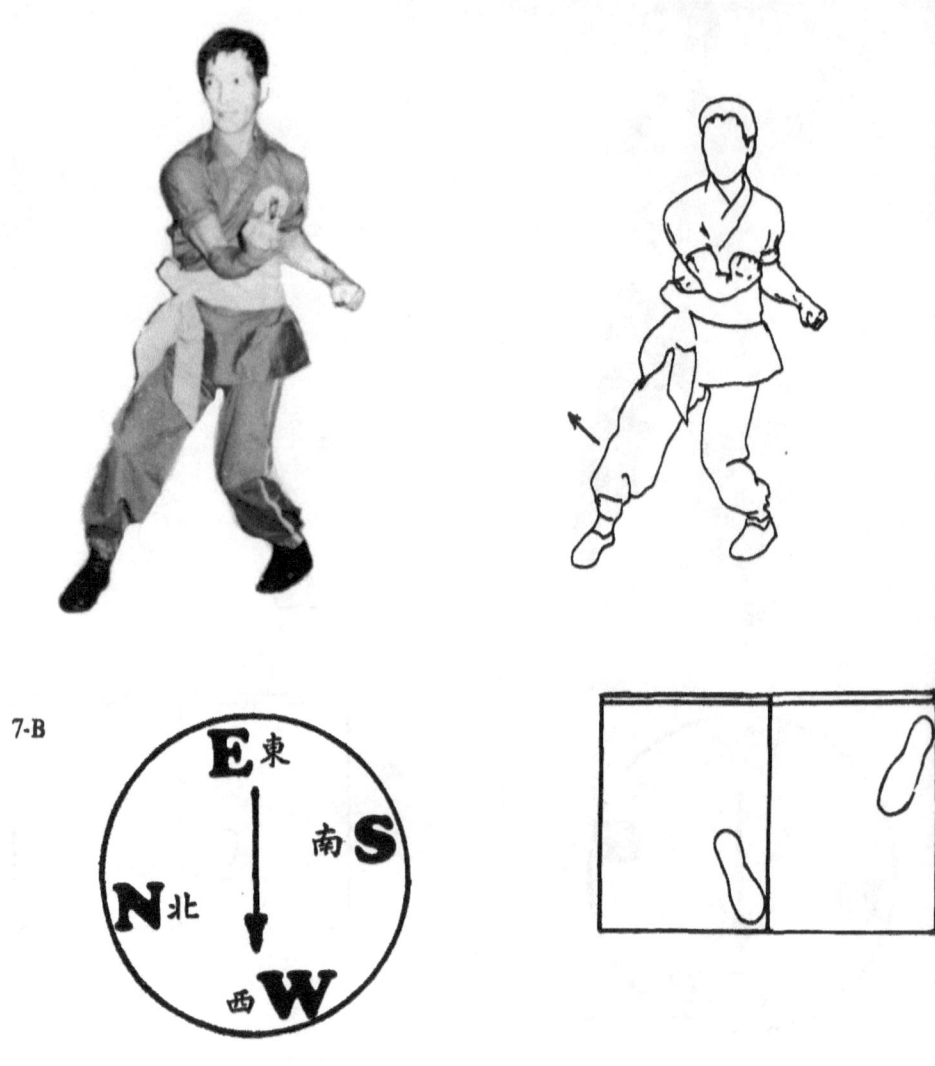

7-B

Pic. 7B : Pull back both hands to the left side of your waist with the left fist facing downward and your right fist facing upward completing the entwining grab technique

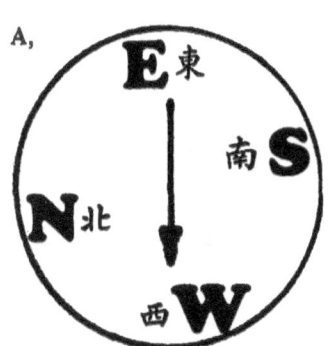
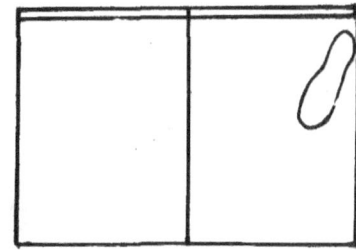

第八式：右足踢
右足踢（側面）

Pic. 8A : Kick with your right foot

8B : Side view of Picture 8.

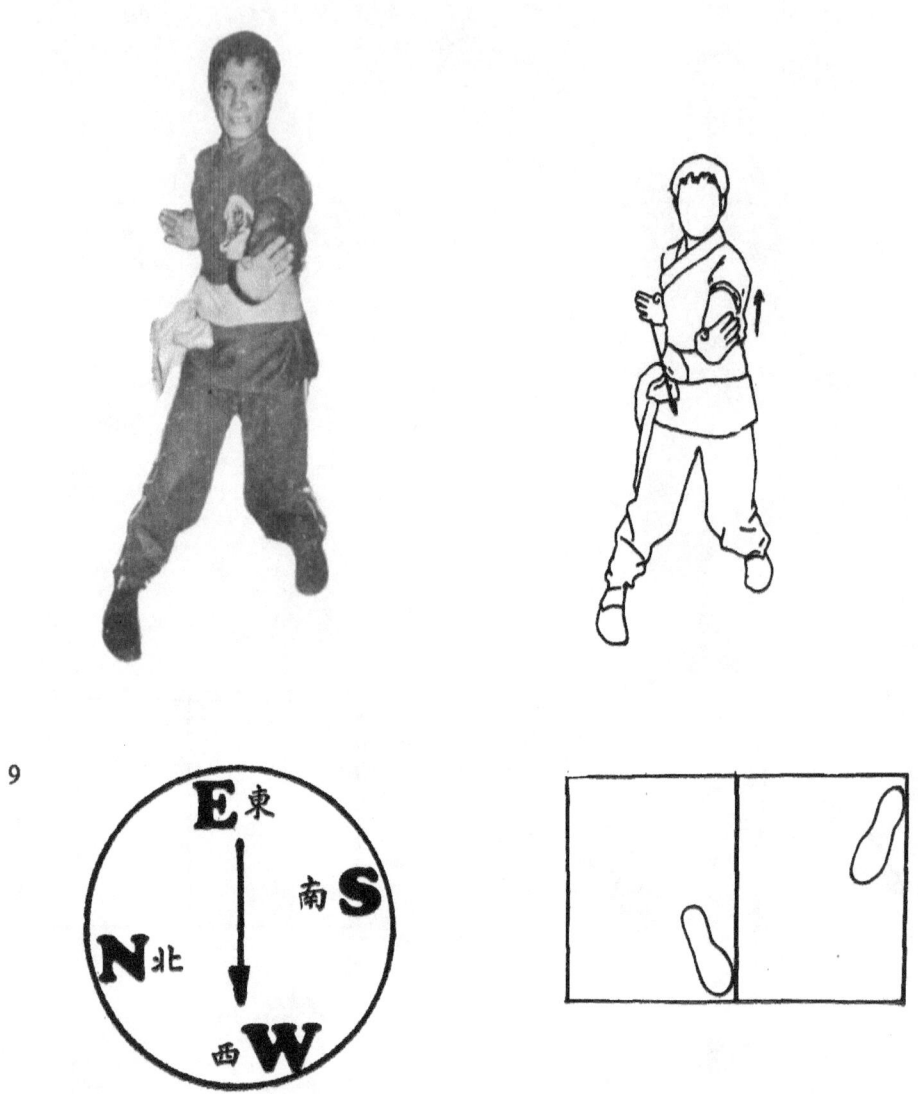

第九式：右足踏前左手掌切

Pic. 9 : Step down with your right foot in a right chian be stance and execute a left slice chop.

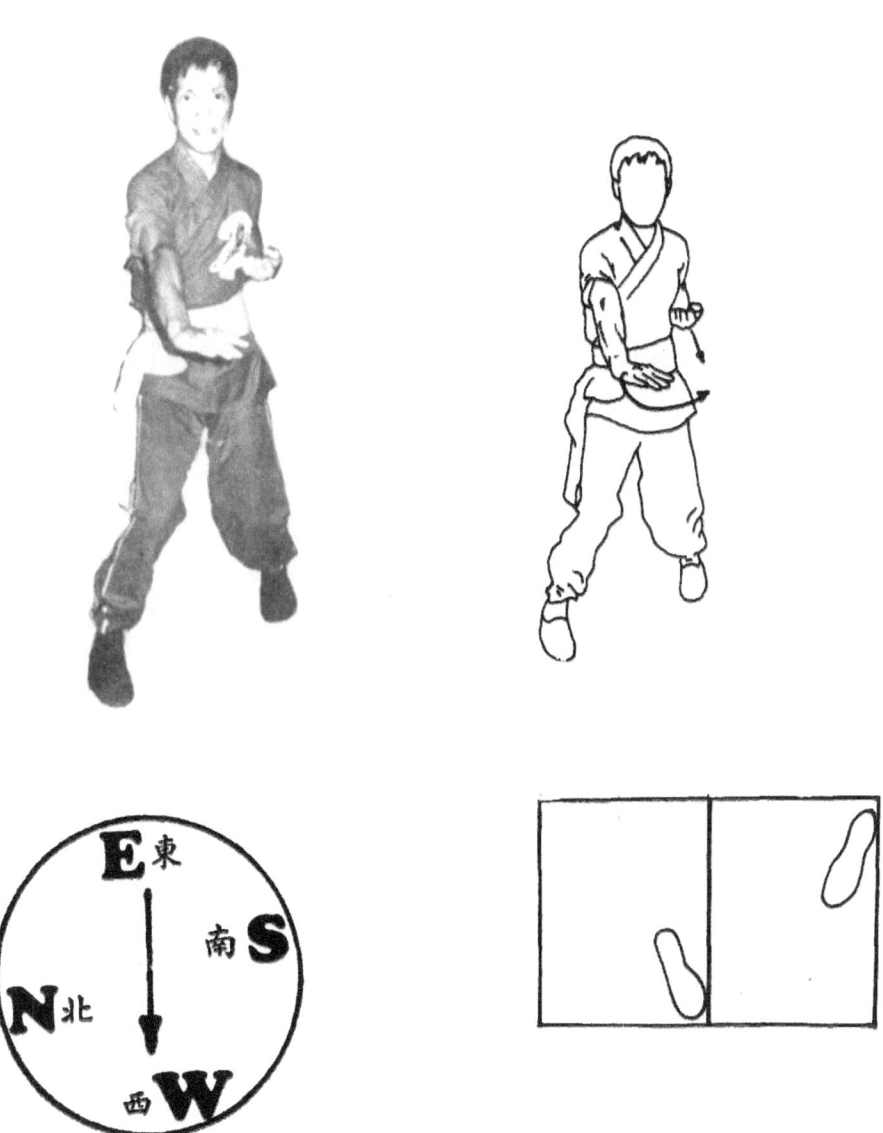

第十式：在馬右手掌剑

Pic. 10 : Execute a right straight side chop

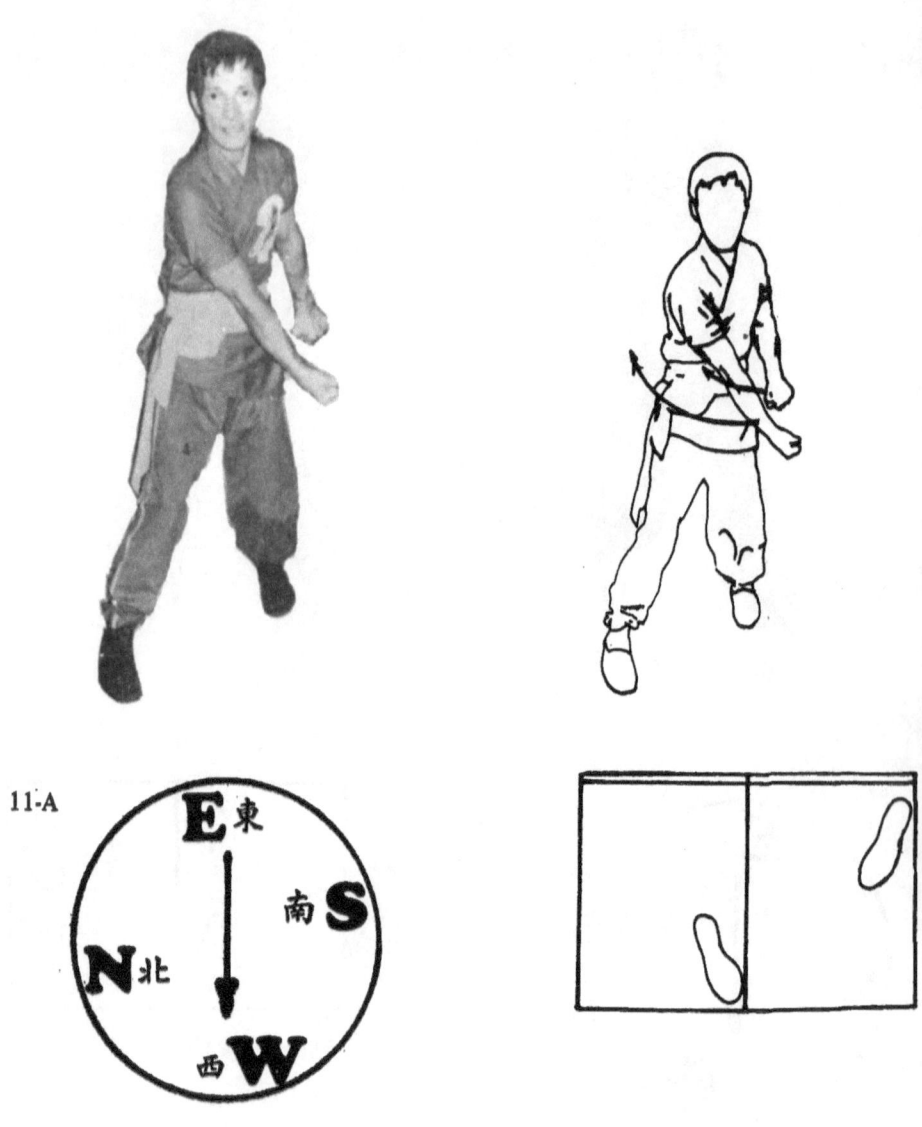

11-A

第十一式：直進右足雙貫中拳第一勢動式

Pic. 11A : Step forward with your right foot with the left leg following by sliding forward in a right chian be stance; clench both fists as you bring them down to your left side

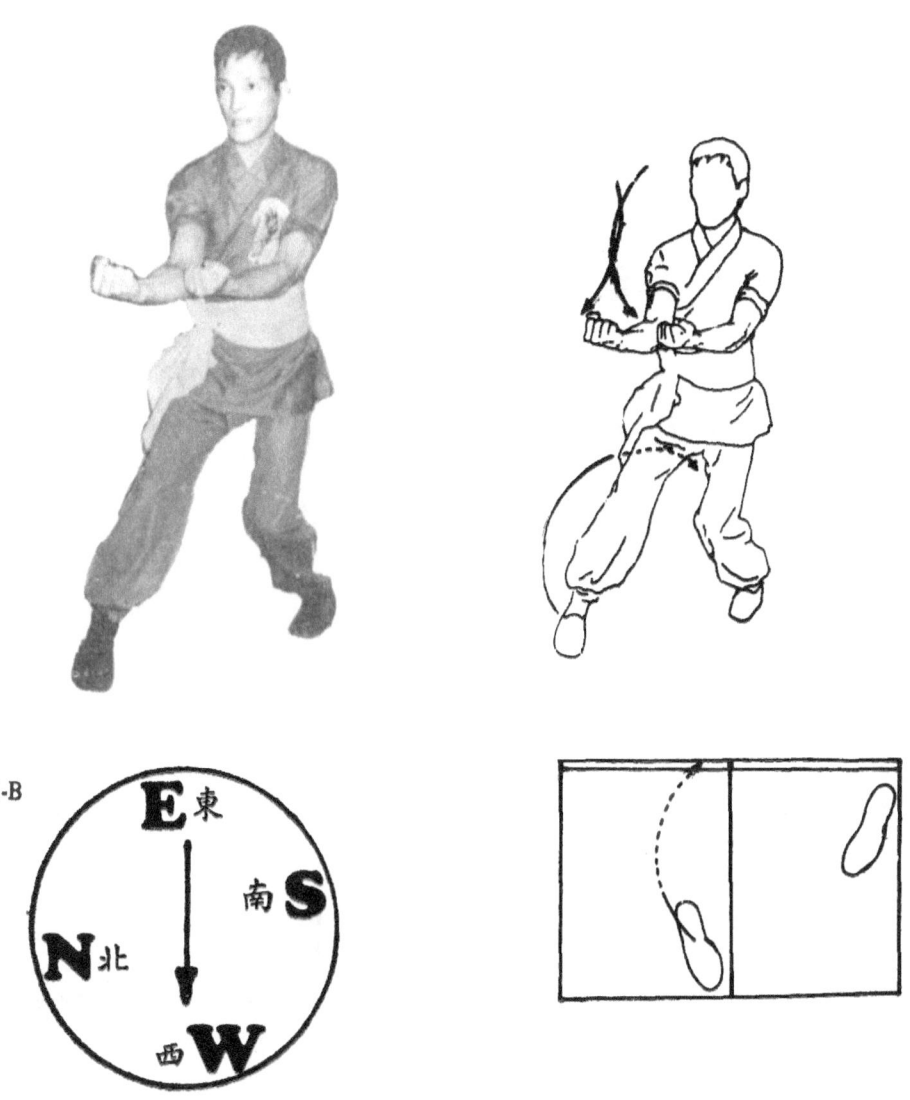

雙貫中拳第二勢定式二勢合一式面向西方

Pic. 11B: Swing both fists upward; execute a double penetrating uppercut.

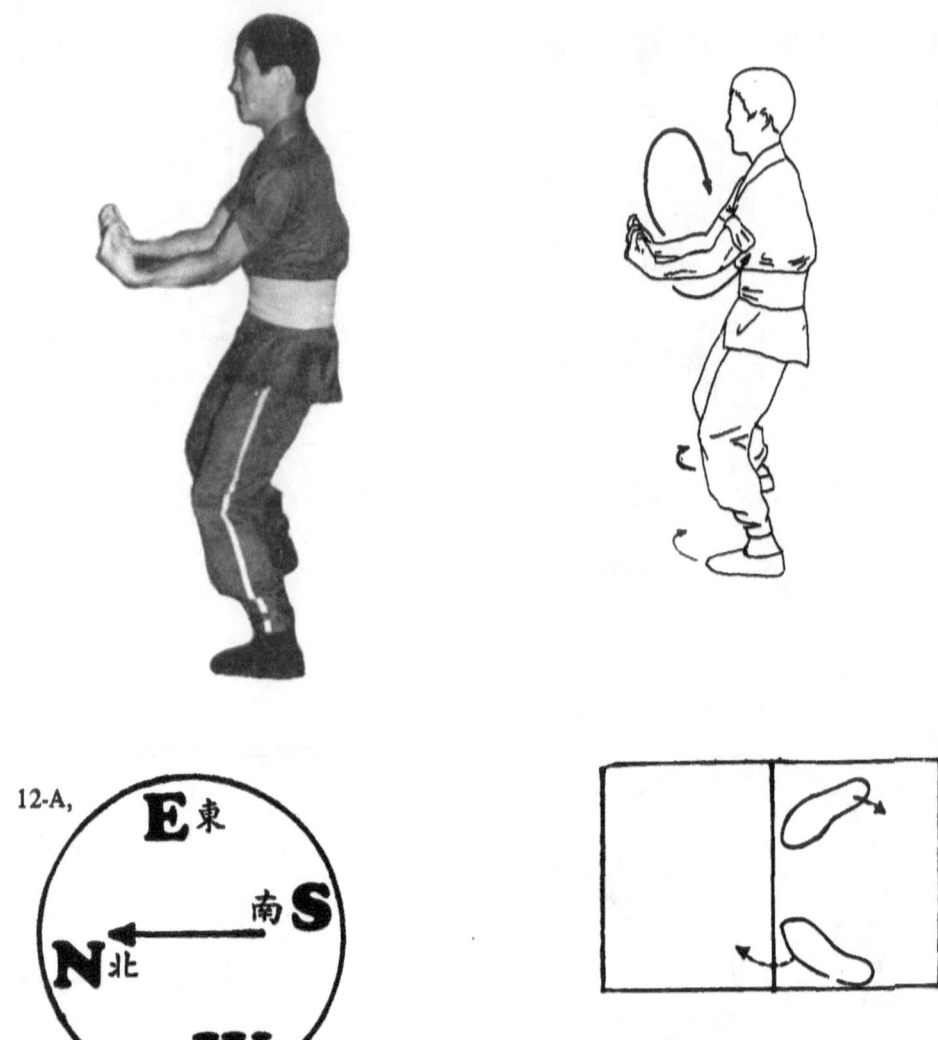

第十二式：退右足轉身向右畔過門向北方雙開錢又名雙鏢

Pic. 12A : Step back with your right leg and turn towards your right facing north (rightside) by stepping with your left leg towards your right; stand in a level stance; execute a double openline block with both fists in a phoenix-eye fist position; bring both hands upward and swing it towards the side of your body.

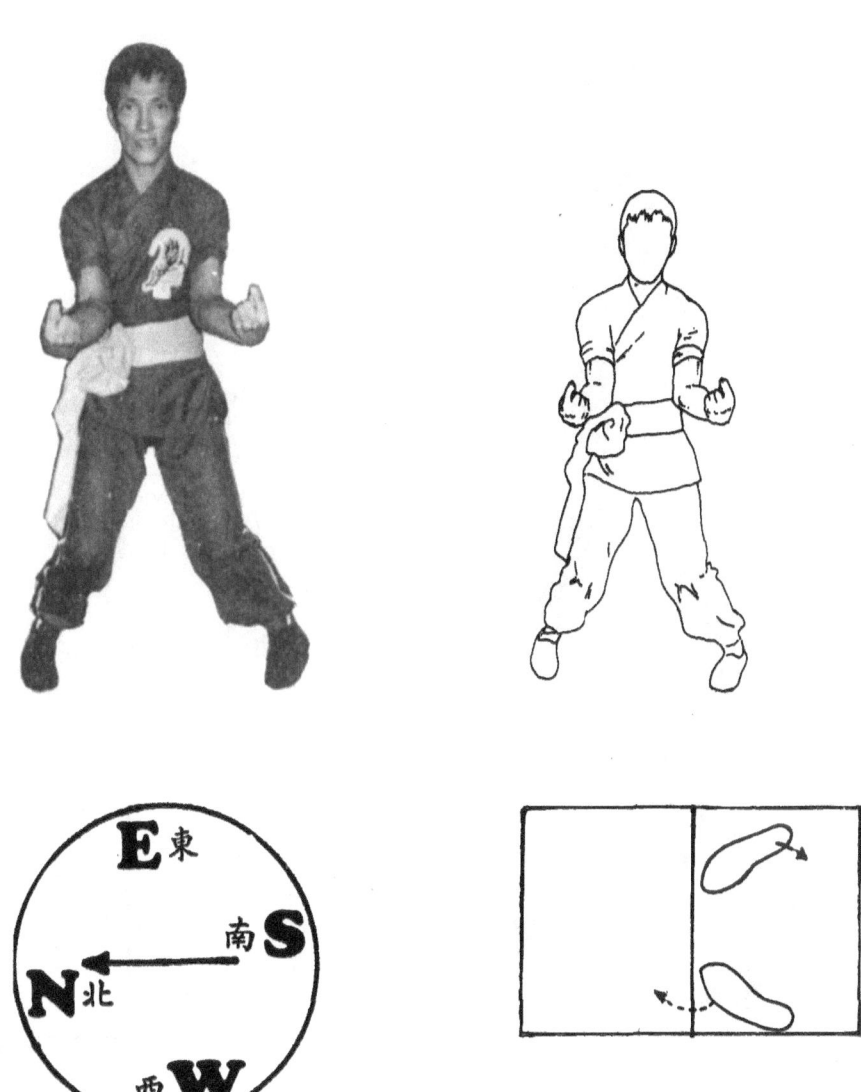

雙開綫（側面）

Pic. 12B : Front view of Pic. 12A.

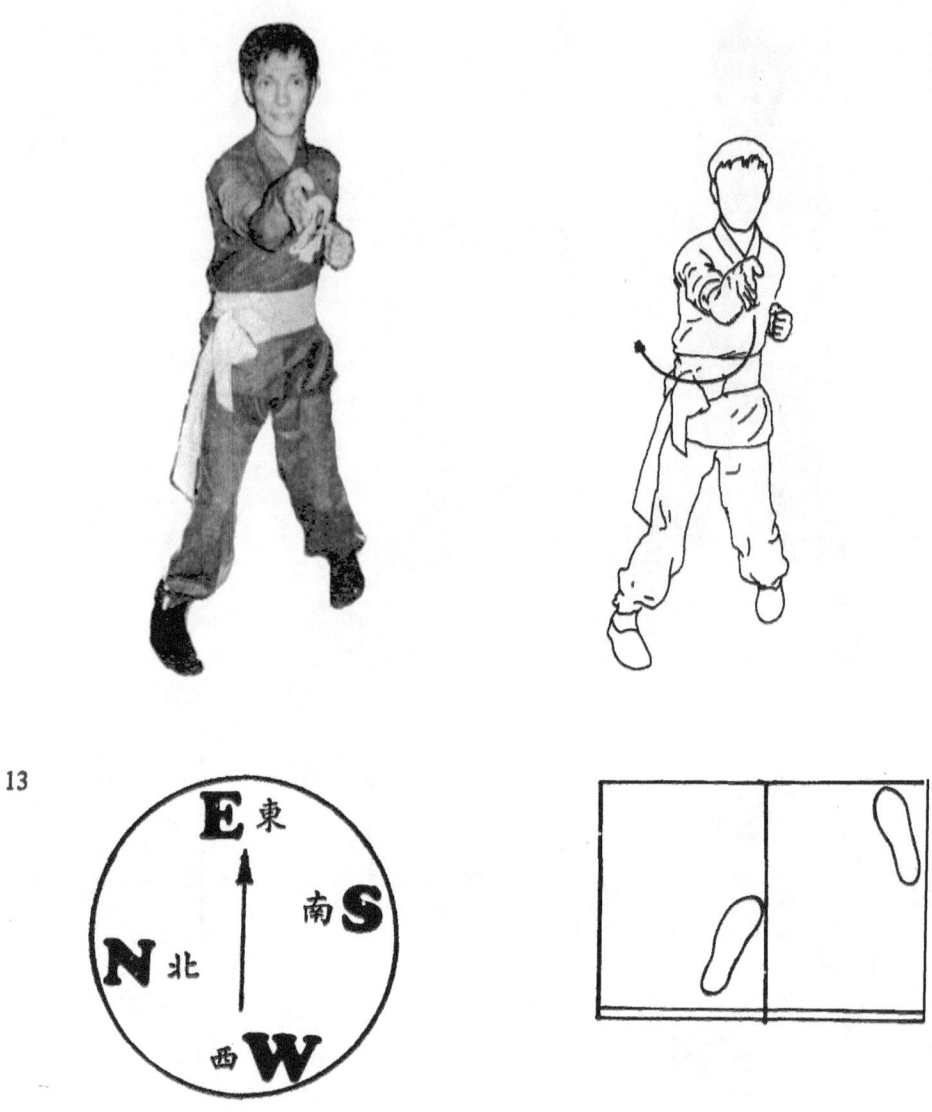

第十三式：轉身向右畔過門向東方踏右足右手掌啄

Pic. 13 : Turn towards your right again, facing East (back) by moving first with your left leg turning towards your right; step forward with your right leg into a right chian be stance and then execute a right finger strike.

第十四式：在馬右手掌蓋

Pic. 14 : Deliver a right scooping block.

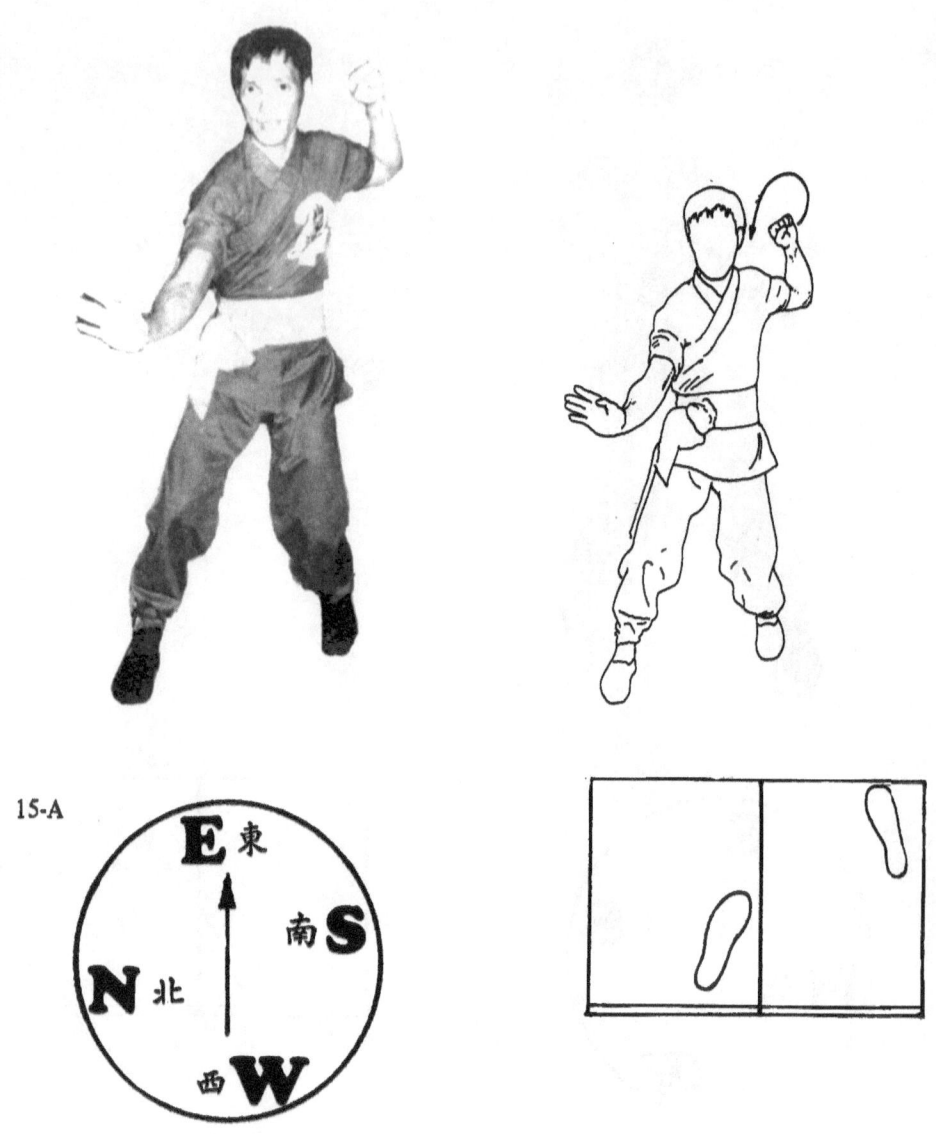

15-A

第十五式：在馬左手握拳鞭勁式第一勢

Pic. 15A : Bring up your left fist beside your head

左手拳鞭定式第二勢二勢合一式

15B: Strike down with a left whip punch (back fist)

第十六式：換馬踏左足左手掌啄

Pic. 16 : Shift stances as you step back with your right leg and step forward with your left leg into a left chian be stance. Execute a left finger strike.

第十七式：在馬左手掌蓋

Pic. 17 : Perform a left scooping block.

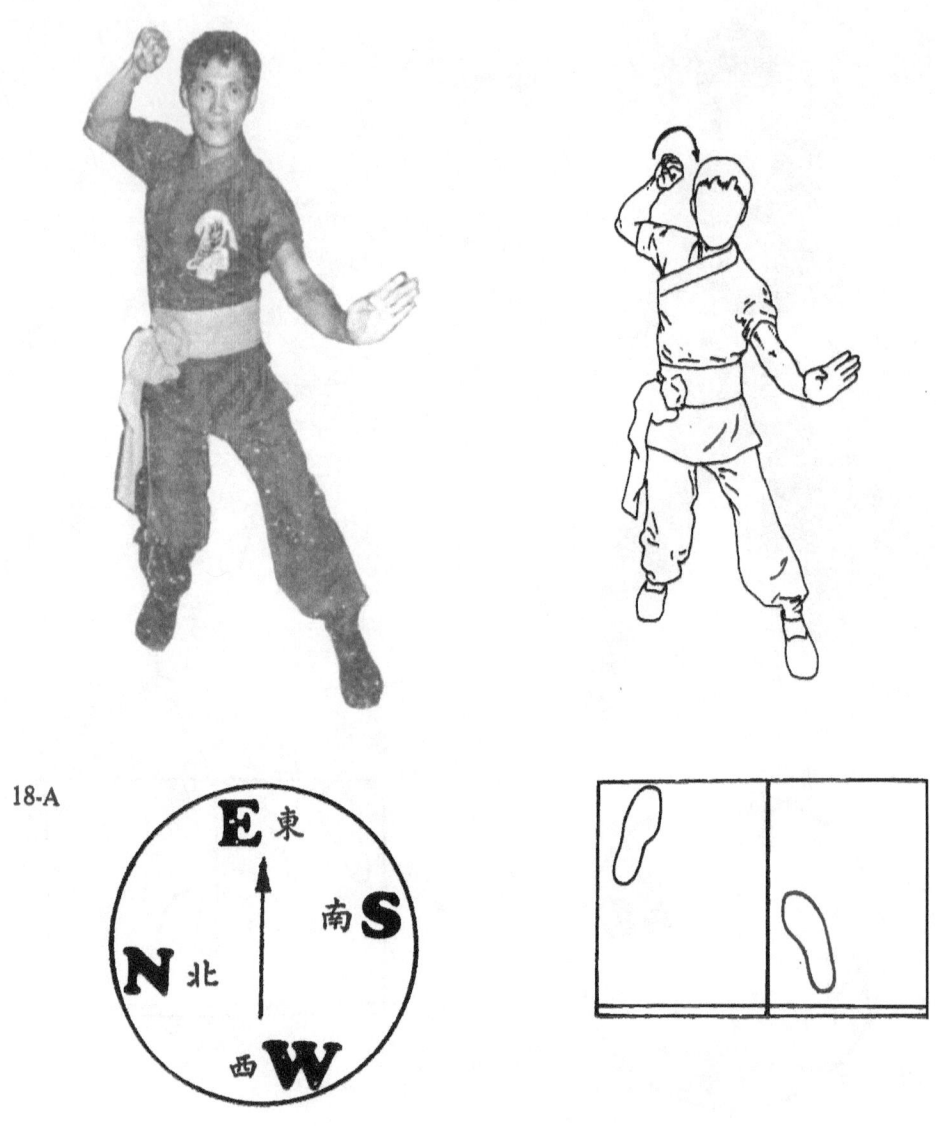

18-A

第十八式：在馬右手握拳鞭勁式第一勢

Pic. 17A : Bring your right fist beside your head

右拳鞭定式第二勢二勢合一式

17B : Strike down with a right whip punch (back fist)

19-A

第十九式：跳進前孩兒抱牌動式第一勢

Pic. 19A : Jump forward with your right leg into a right toe stance and execute

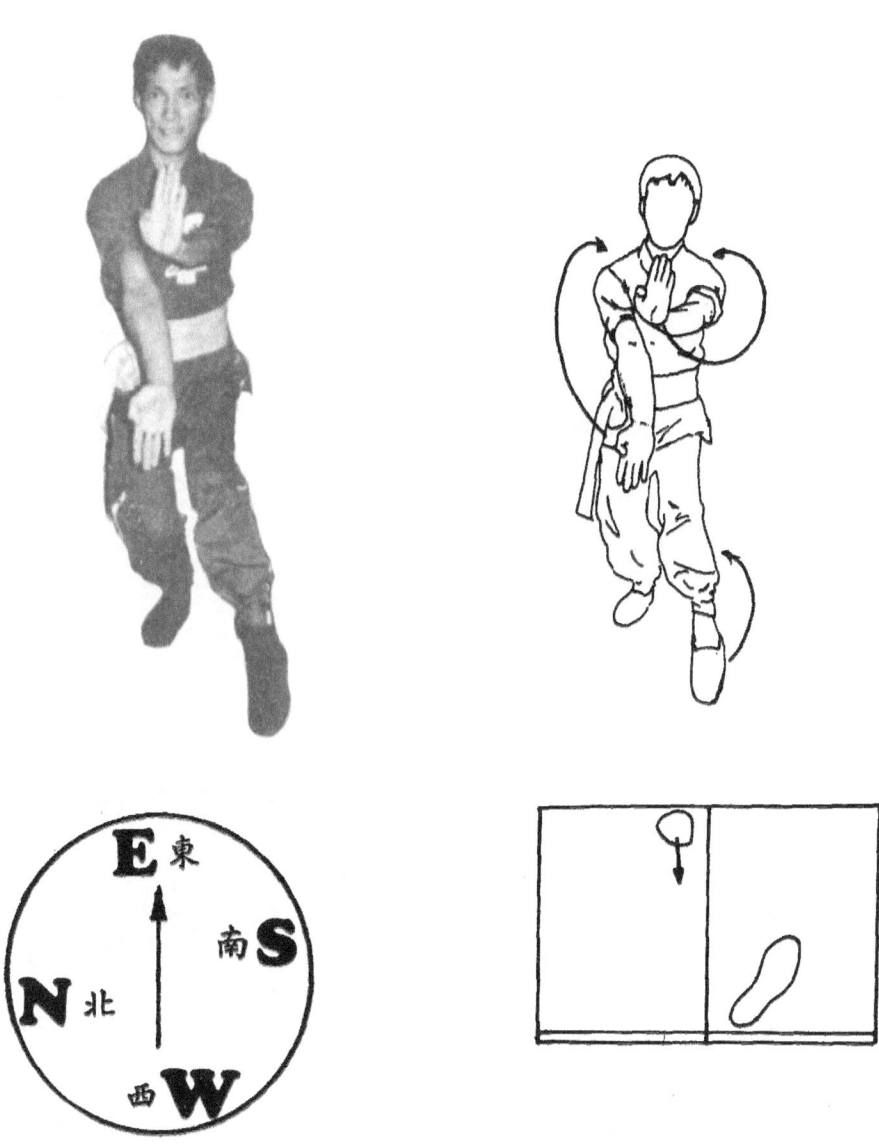

跳進前審左足孩兒抱牌擋第二勢定式二勢合一式

19B : "Children holding the tablet" palm strike

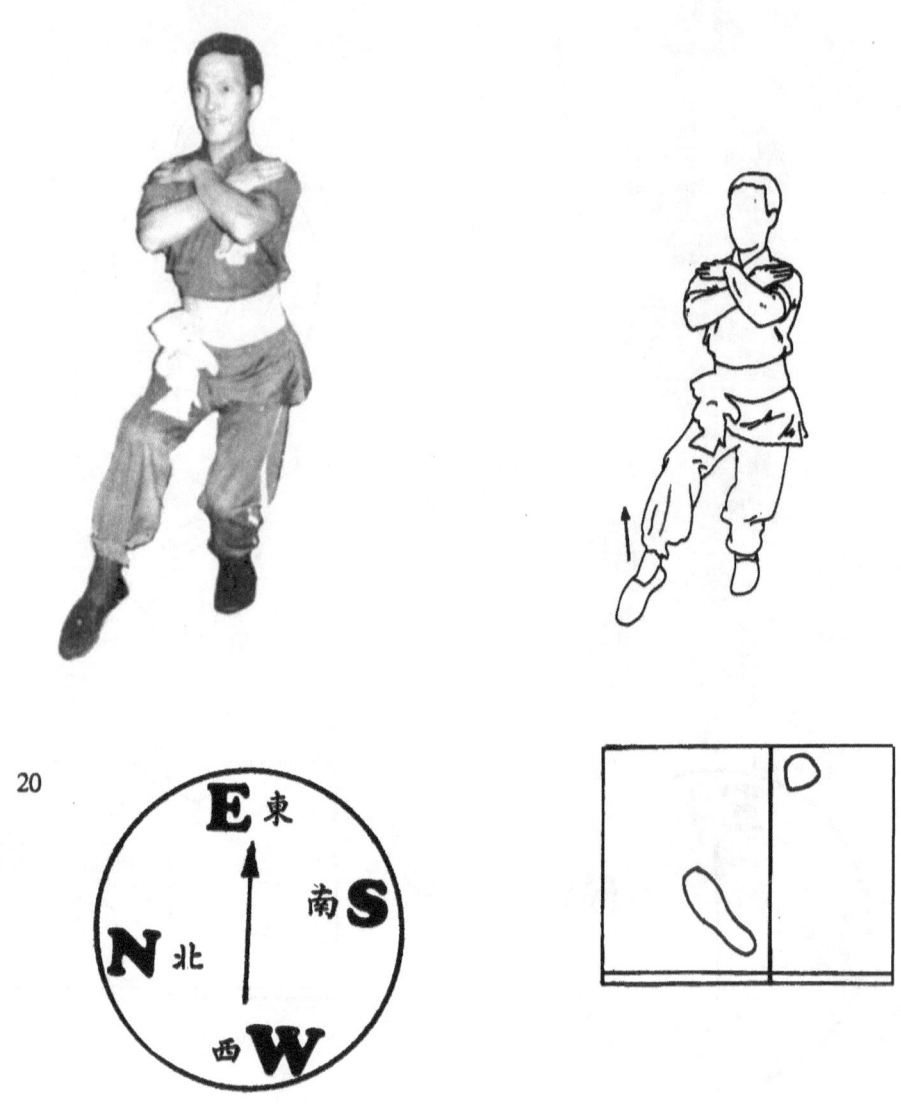

第二十式：跳退後寄右足雙扯胸

Pic. 20 : Jump backwards with your right leg into a left toe stance and perform a cross hand covering block.

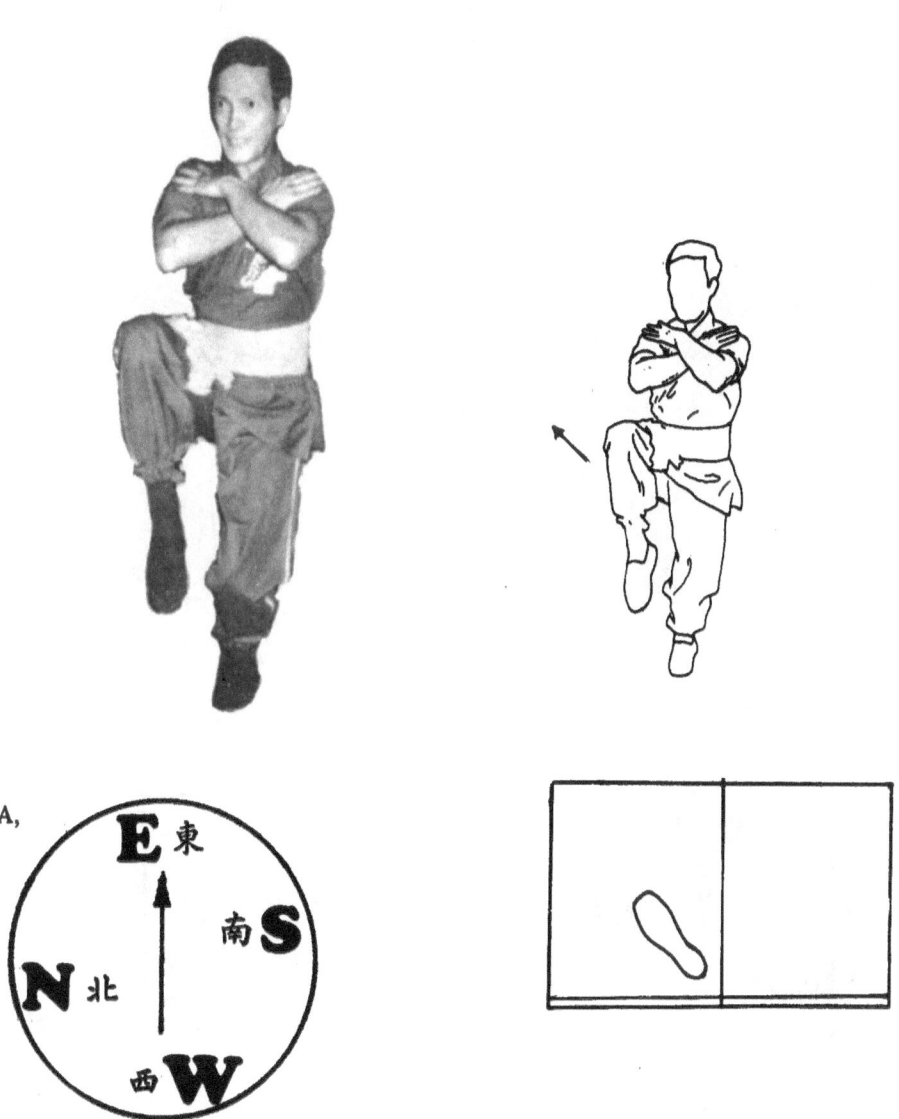

第廿一式：踢右足動式第一勢

Pic. 21A : Kick with your right foot

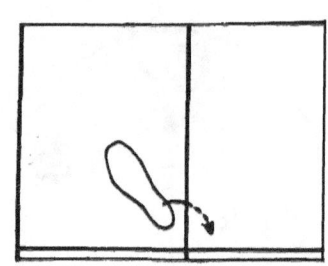

踢右足定式第二勢二勢合一式面向東方

21B

第廿二式：右足退後一步左足退楣右足俊轉右畔面向南方
觀音坐運第一勢。

Pic. 22A: Step backward with your right leg as your left leg follows into a crossed stance and bring both palms upward

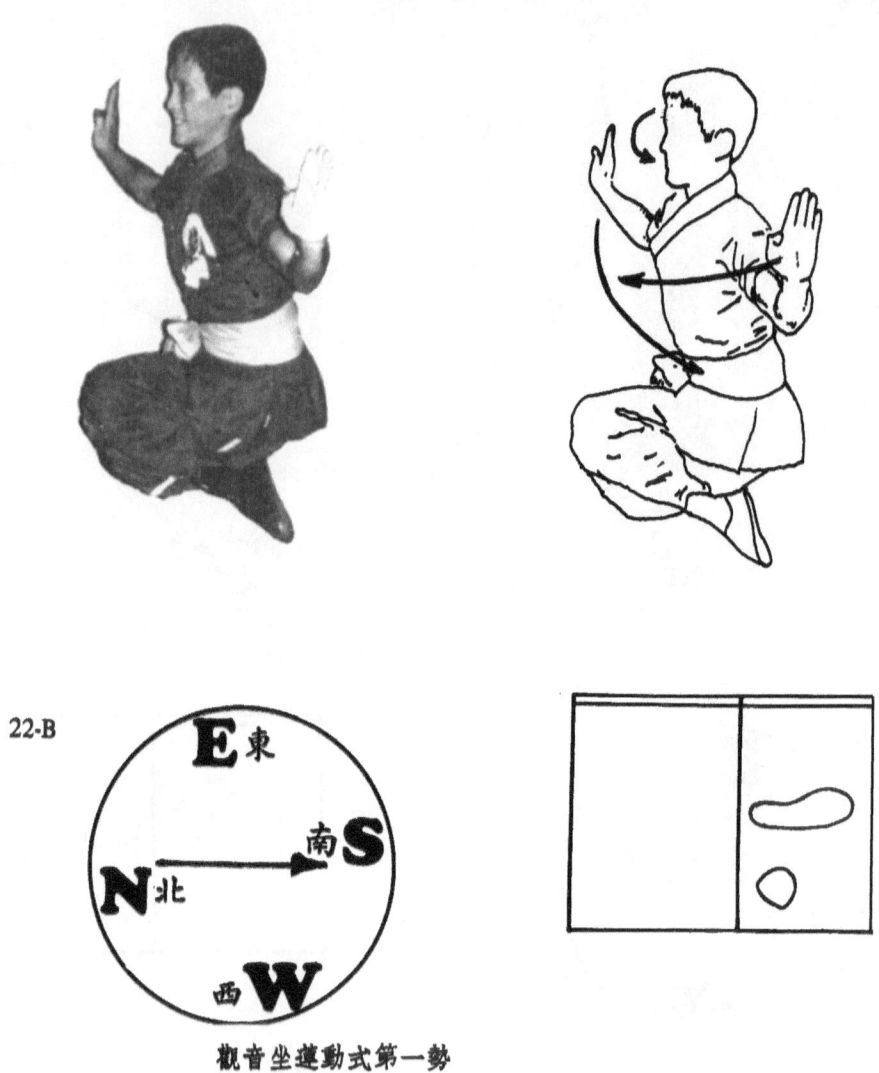

22-B

觀音坐蓮動式第一勢
觀音坐蓮定式第二勢面向南方二勢合一式

Pic. 22B : Kneel down with your crossed leg into a lotus stance as you chop down with both palms.

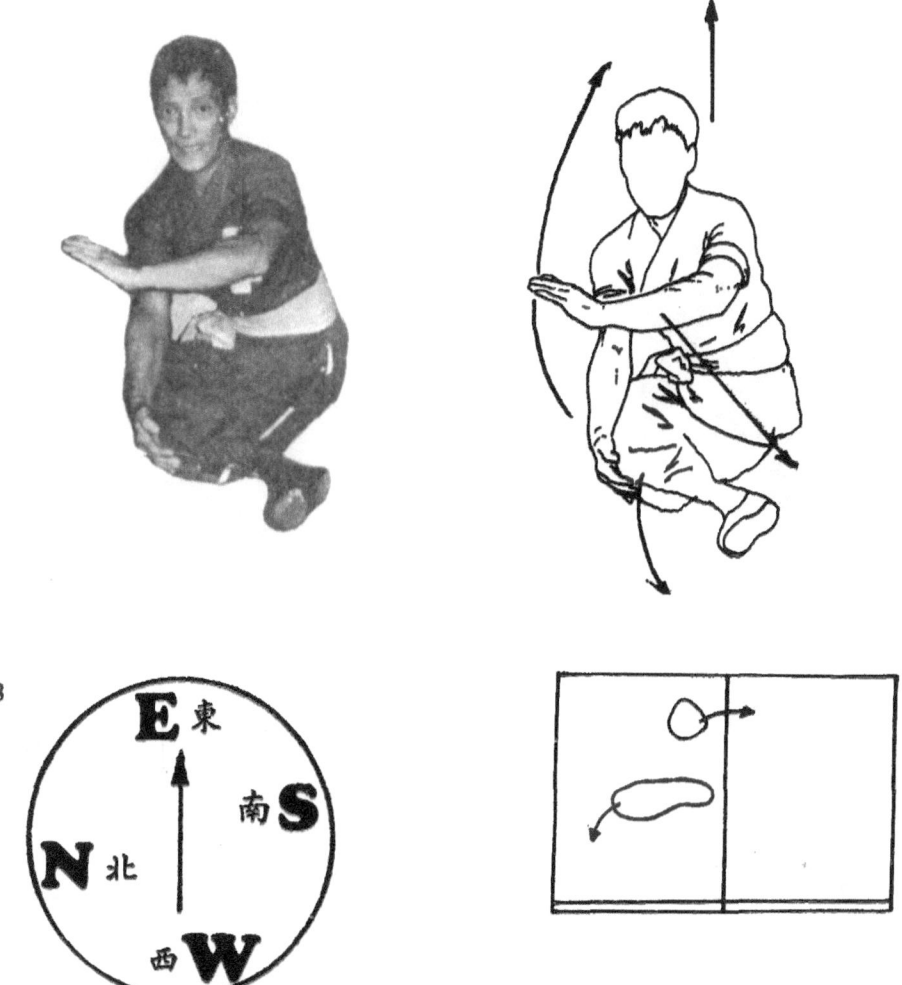

第廿三式：轉左畔呈身向東方力士搏

Pic. 23 : Facing towards your left, extend your right palm forward with the left palm pushing down, as you pull back with your right hand, performing the ground grabbing techques.

24-A.

第廿四式：踏右足右手搨動式第一勢面向東方

Pic. 24A : As you pull your right hand into the right side of your head, press down your left hand into a left openhand downward block position. Stand up with the right leg forward in a right chian be stance

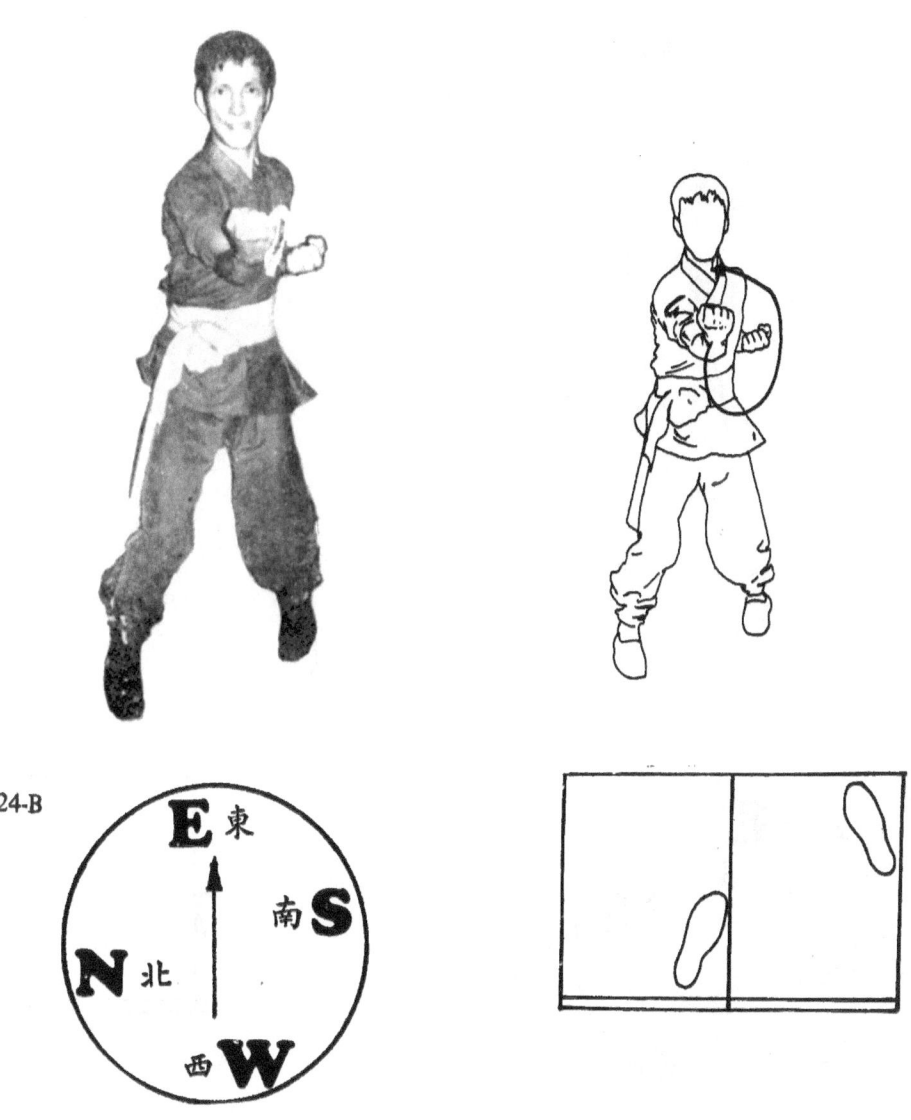

24-B

踏右足右手擂定式第二勢向東方二勢合一式

Pic. 24B : With your right fist, strike down with a hammer strike.

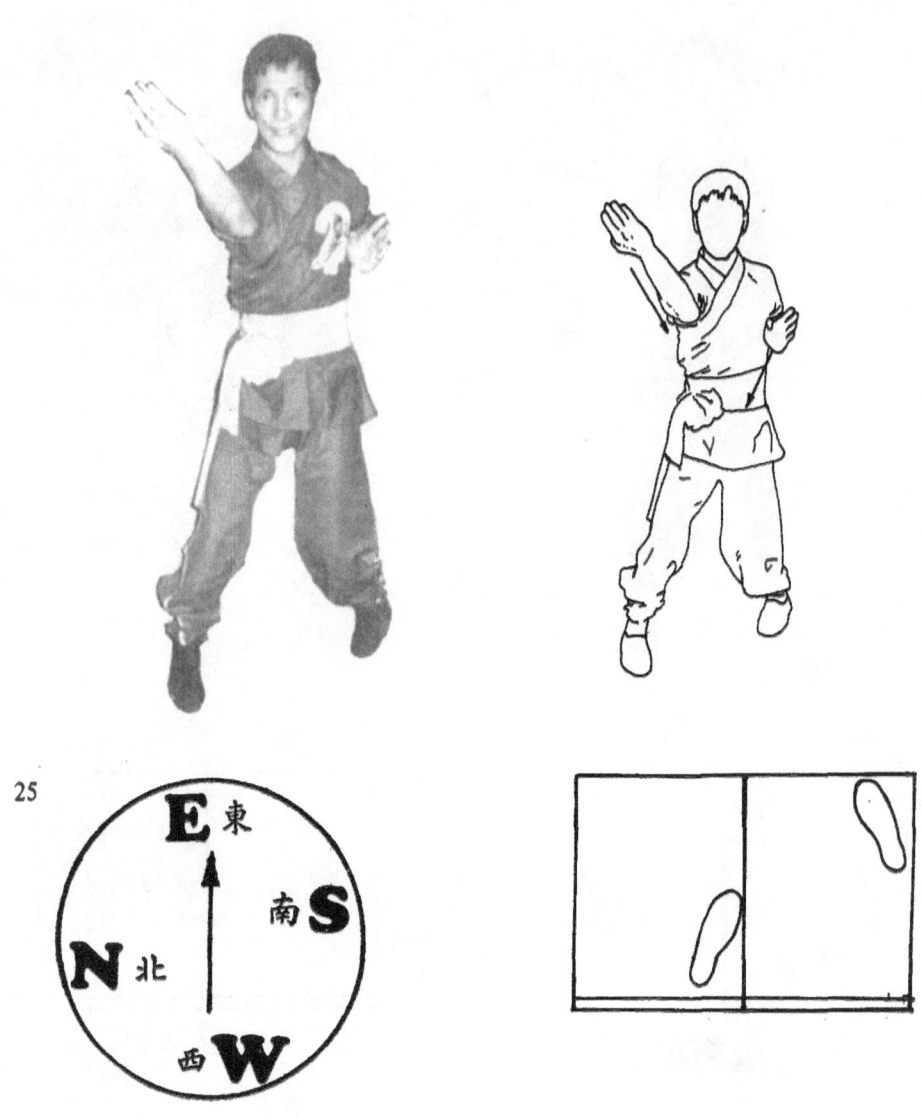

第廿五式：踏右足右手掌挑向東方

Pic. 25 : Execute a right open hand outside block facing east (back).

第廿六式：踏右足左手掌切向東方

Pic. 26 : Deliver a left slice chop

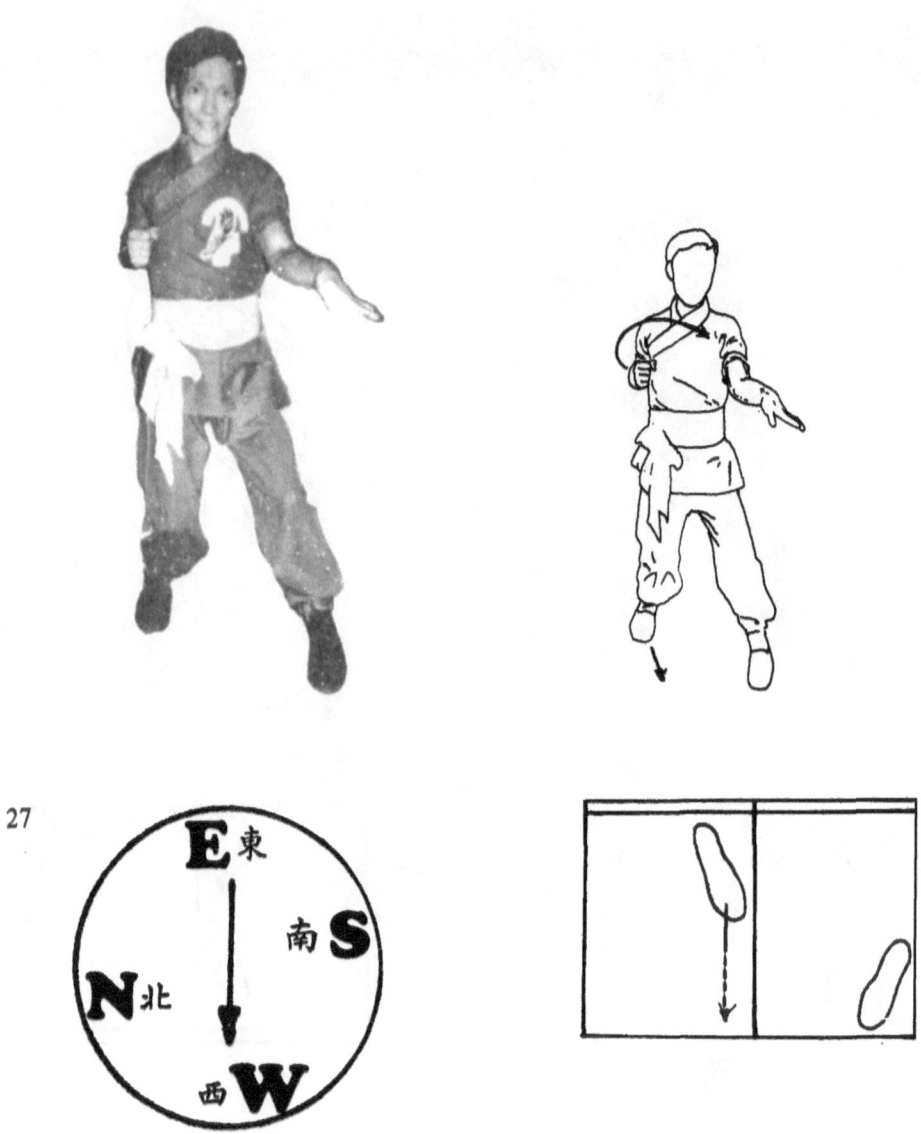

第廿七式：左轉身翻後過門向西方踏左足左、擒

Pic. 27 : Pivot towards your left side 180° so that your face west (forward) by stepping towards your left with your right leg. Turn your left leg so that you stand in a left chian-be stance. Execute a left grabbing block.

第廿八式：踏右足打肘面向西方

Pic. 28 : Step forward with your right leg into a right chian be stance. Hit your palm with your right elbow.

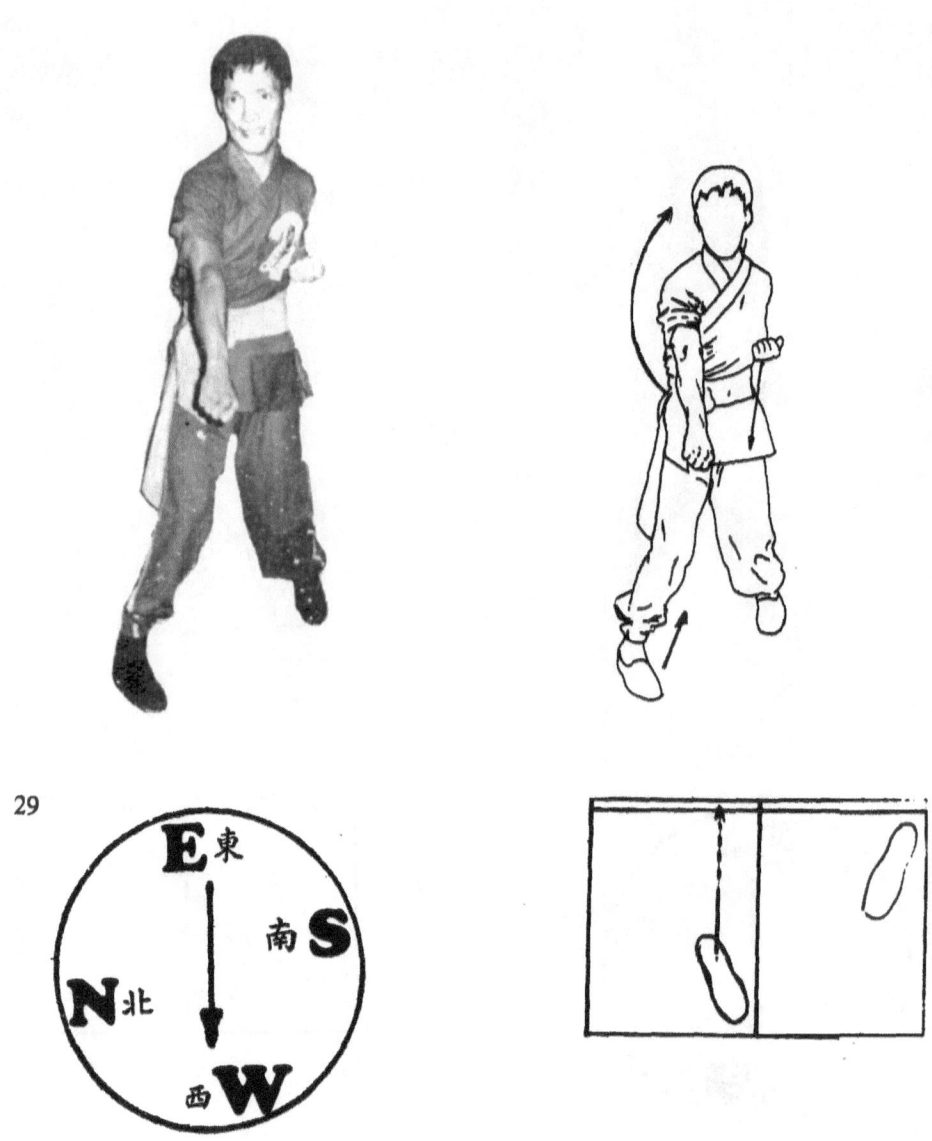

第廿九式：在馬右手反墜拳

Pic. 29 : From the position of the elbow strike, punch downward with your right fist in an inverted position.

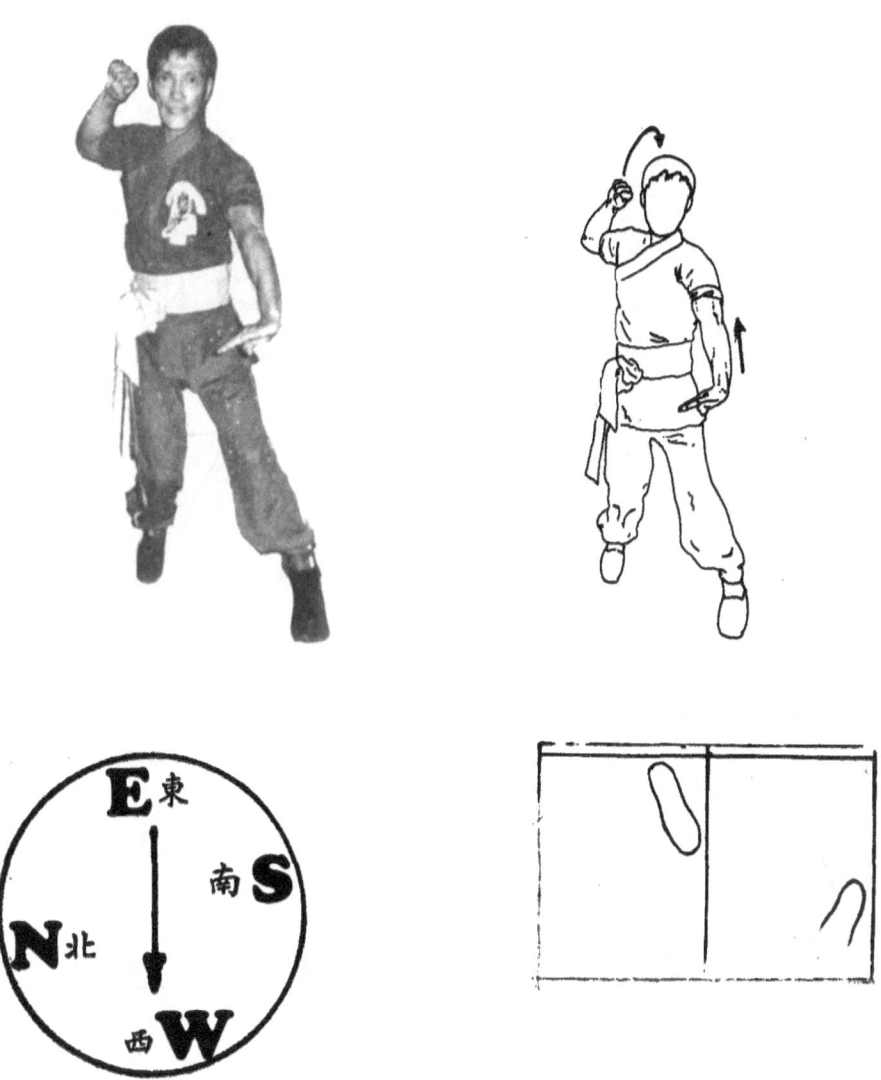

第三十式：退右足左手掌開向西方

Pic. 30 : Step back with your right leg into a left chian be stance. Perform a left open hand downward block.

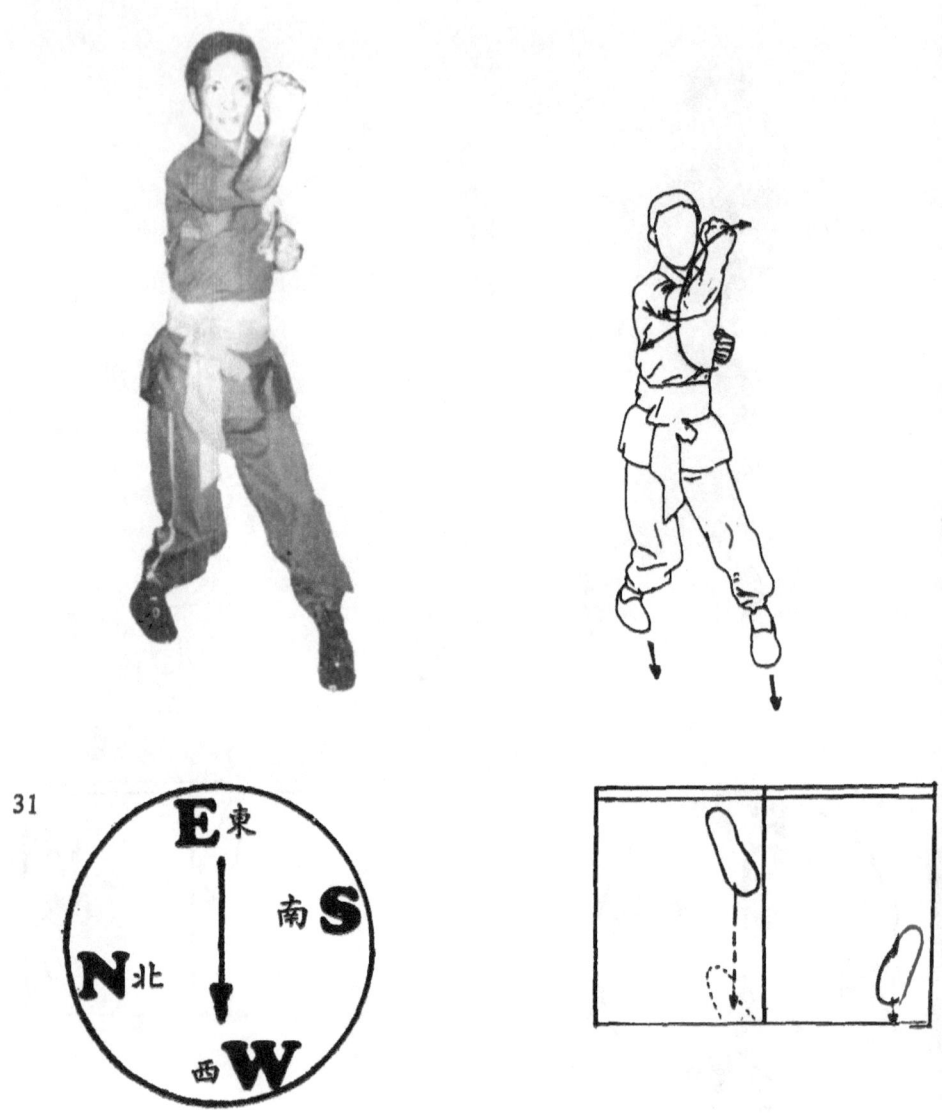

第卅一式：在馬右手拳鞭向西方

Pic. 31 : Strike down with a right whip punch (backfist)

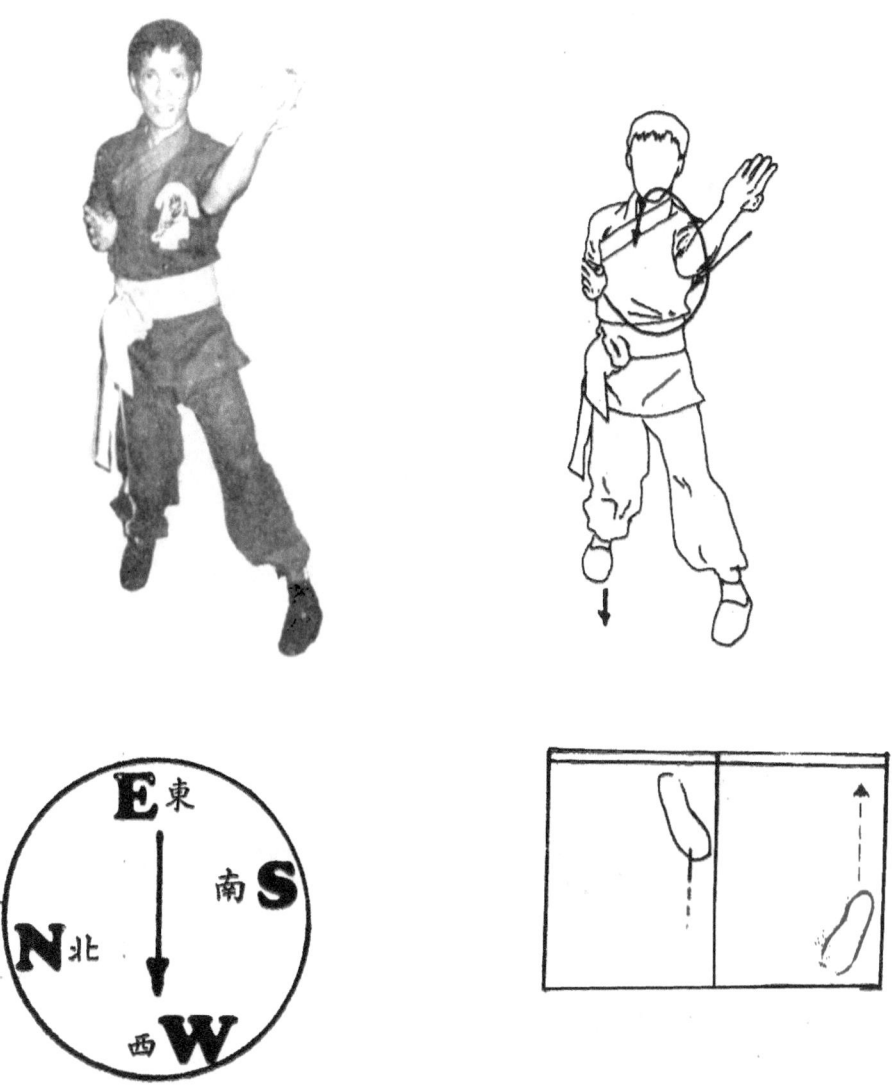

第卅二式：雙疊進左足左手掌挑
（先進右足　再進左足）

Pic. 32 : Double step forward by first stepping forward with your right foot, and then stepping forward again with your left foot into a left chian be stance. Deliver a left open hand outside block.

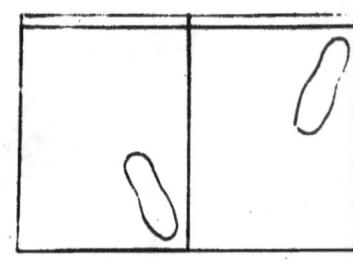

第卅三式：換馬踏右足右手掌風鼓劈
退馬寄右足招陽手收式正面向西方

33 : Change stance by stepping back with left leg and then step forward with your right leg and execute a right downward chop with your right hand.

Step back into a right toe stance and close the form by using the chiao-yong closing hand.

2

## 達尊法　茵籐踢：　　用法

（第二式，三式用法　走馬閃右，左手開；右手切）
　第二式：甲方踏左馬，左拳貫中拳擊乙方胸部
　第三式：乙方走馬閃右邊，左手開並用右掌切擊甲方腰側
（第四，五式用法　走馬閃左，右手開，左手切）
　第四式：甲方踏右馬，右拳貫中乙方胸部
　第五式：乙方走馬閃左邊，右手開並用左掌切擊甲方腰側
　　　（第六式用法　踏左足，左手擒）

### 3.
### Application of TAMO'S METHOD ENTWINING KICK

Application of Left Open Hand Downward Block, Right Slice Chop (Pic. 2 & 3)

Pic.   A punches B with his left fist; B sidesteps into his left side and blocks with a right openhand downward block

Pic.   B counters with a left slice chop into A's waist

4

6

第六式：甲方踏右馬，右拳貫中擊乙方胸部，乙方踏左足，左手擒甲方右手腕

**Application of Left Grabbing Block (kim) (Pic. 6)**

Pic.  A punches B with his right fist; B blocks the punch with his left hand and grab A's arm at the elbow, controlling A's right arm

7-A

（第七式，八式用法　茵簾手梭，右足踢）
第七式：甲方左拳擊乙方胸部，乙方用茵簾手梭甲方左拳
甲方退左脚右手拳脫開乙方茵簾手

Application of the Entwining Grab (Pic. 7A & B)

Pic.   A punches B with his left fist; B blocks the punch by using both hands, the right hand grabbing at A's elbow joint, the left hand grabbing at A's wrist. By twisting both arms and pulling them back, B could drag A forward to the ground, completing the entwining grab technique.

7-B

8

第八式：乙方起右腿踢甲方下腹

Application for Entwining Kick (Pic. 8)

Pic.   A steps back with his left foot and uses a right downward block to break away from B's entwining grab

Pic.   B immediately counters with a right kick into A's abdomen

11-A

(第十一式：用法 雙貫中拳)
第十一式：甲方右拳擊乙方胸部，乙方右拳開
乙方收勢進馬用雙貫中拳擊甲方腹部

Pic. A punches B with his right fist; B blocks the punch with a right downward block

Pic. and slide forward with his right leg and delivers a double penetrating uppercut into A's stomach

12

（第十二式用法　雙開鉞又名雙標）
第十二式：甲方踏右馬用葫蘆手攻擊乙方兩腰側
　　　　　乙方踏平馬用鳳眼指雙開鉞標開

**Application of the Open Line Block (Pic. 12A)**

Pic.　A attack B's waist by using a double hook punch; B blocks the punch thrusting outward both hands, the fist in a phoenix eye fist position curled upward to tense the forearm, pressing down on A's both hands

13

（第十三式用法　右手掌啄）
　　第十三式：甲方右拳擊乙方胸部，乙方踏右馬，右手解甲方右拳，連打啄，插甲方胸部

Application of the Right Finger Strike (Pic. 13)

Pic.　A punches B with his right fist; B blocks the punch with his right forearm and poke A's solar plexus with his right finger strike

（第十四，十五式用法　右手掌蓋，左拳鞭）
　　第十四式：甲方用鈎搖拳搖擊乙方腹部，乙方踏右馬用右掌轉蓋開

Application of the Right Scooping Block (Pic. 14)

Pic.　A attacks B with a right uppercut; B blocks the punch with a scooping block by circling his right arm in a counterclockwise circle then sliding under A's right arm. B could easily lock A's arm by squeezing his right forearm upward into his biceps, locking A's arm.

14

第十五式：乙方用左拳鞭甲方面中

15

**Application of Left Whip Punch (Pic. 15A & B)**

Pic.   After the scooping block. B counters with a left whip punch into A's face

19

（第十九式用法　寄左足孩兒抱牌擋）
第十九式：跳進寄足步孩兒抱牌式推擋敵人胸腹部）
（第廿式，廿一式用法　寄右足雙扯胸，踢右足
第廿，廿一式：甲方起右腿踢乙方，乙方用雙扯胸式解甲方右踢，同時起右腳踢甲方下陰

Application of "Child Holding the Tablet" Palm Strike (Pic. 19A & B)

Pic.　B jumps forward into a right hanging stance and strikes with both palms hitting A's chest and stomach area. The position of the hands resemble the gesture holding a tablet, thus the name "holding the tablet" palm strike

Application of Cross Hand Covering Block, Right Kick (Pic. 20 & 21)

Pic.　A kicks B with a right front kick, B blocks the kick with a cross hand covering block by crossing both arms infront of his chest blocking A's kick. B counters with a right kick to A's groin.

20-21

22

23-A

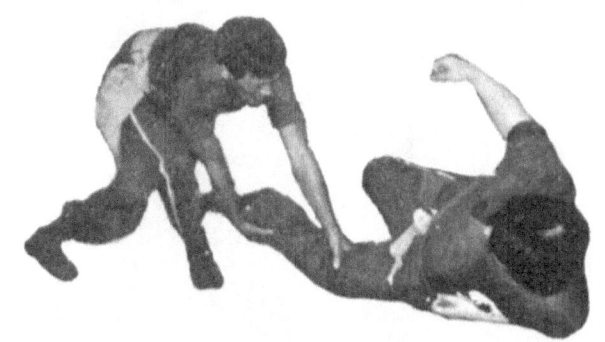

23-B

（第廿二，廿三式用法　觀音坐蓮，力士擋）
　第廿二式：乙方觀音坐蓮式，甲方踏左足準備右拳擊乙方面中
　第廿三式：甲方右拳撞出時，乙方變力士擋式拼甲方左脚，使甲方跌撲
（第廿四式用法　右手拳頂）
　第廿四式：乙方踏左馬左手掌開敵人右拳，右手拳頂敵人胸部

Application of Lotus Stance, Ground Grabbing Technique (Pic. 22 & 23)

Pic.　B is in the lotus stance; A prepares to punch B

Pic.　As A punches B, B uses the ground grabbing technique by pulling and grabbing A's left ankle with his right hand, and striking A's knee with his left palm

Pic.　B continue pulling and pressing both arms into A's left leg throwing A to the ground.

Application of the Right Hammer Strike (Pic. 24A & B)

Pic.　A punches B with his right fist; B blocks the punch with a left open hand downward block and hit A's chest with a right hammer strike

28

29

（第廿八式，廿九式用法　打節，反墜拳）
　第廿八式：乙方進右馬打短節擊甲方胸部，甲方用盤轉手式盤折乙方
　　　　　　右手肘節
　第廿九式：乙方用挨式反墜拳擊甲方腹部
（第卅三式：風鼓劈）
　第卅三式：甲方踏右馬右拳撞擊乙方，乙方踏右馬，右手掌用風鼓劈
　　　　　　式，劈擊甲方面部速解帶攻

Application of Right Elbow Strike, Inverted Punch (Pic. 28,29)

Pic.　B attacks A with a right elbow strike; A blocks the strike by grabbing B's wrist and elbow, twisting them towards the right in a clockwise circle to break B's arm

Pic.　B follows with a twisting action and delivers an inverted punch into A's abdomen

Application of Right Downward Chop (Pic. 33)

PIc.　A steps forward to deliver a punch to B's face; B side steps to his left, blocks A's punch with his right forearm and chops down into A's face

Pic: 1. The Lohan Tiger subduing technique

## 雙短鞭羅漢伏虎勢
## 護身雙短鞭

雙短鞭為本派師祖所創設流傳至今將近九十年，為獨特武器，我國武林中鮮見此種兵器，但在福建晉南五縣及漳厦一帶則甚風行，因其輕便，出遠門插在腰間亦可作防身禦敵之用。

雙短鞭法共有四套，可單練，亦可對拆棍或斬馬刀。

# CHAPTER VIII - WEAPONS

## 論拳與械

### 顏振城

　　凡欲練武術。必先學善性。善性乃能柔。柔克己。能柔則所見者遠。所成者大。「不怒於私敵。而勇於公敵。不怒於私仇。而勇於國仇」。不怕難而中止。不見辱而拔劍。因愛身而愛國愛軍。為強己而強國強種。此吾人之職務也。續以精拳術者。應當兼習器械。有時遇敵固可以空拳徒手。應對裕如。若遇對方。械精器良。恐非徒手所能了之也。

　　考弓矢時代。器械種甚多。分別之惟以木與鐵製成者。木棍。南方曰槌仔。有丈二。九尺。七尺。齊眉等。練習時須。站丁八馬一條身。弒持平為硬子午姿勢。馬進退分清。左右有勢。自然有力。勢敗則力無由而展矣。槌有軟法。有硬法。有上下槌。單頭槌。雙頭槌之分。宋太祖連拳祖師之槌。槌也。魯班祖師上身槌。亦屬硬槌之用法。最常實中破敵。除打挾閃之攻勢。如猛虎下山。瀑布直瀉。力勢甚雄。犯者披廓。偷敵人閃避不得。被其所算。鮮免受其重傷。而羅漢槌。白鶴槌。猴槌均為柔軟之槌也。用法應勢而入。對於中門攻入。不足敗敵。如分左右斜轉。乘虛而入。以柔制剛。取勝之道。在乎是矣。諺云四兩可破千斤。卻此意也。槌法不論軟硬務須謹慎上中下左右五門。勿輕放鬆為要。

　　鐵器製成者。曰刀。曰劍。叉鈀鞭鐧。鉤鐮等。難以盡述。

　　師祖所創設五祖器械法。長兵器有關刀斬馬刀。梅花槍。方天戟。鉤鐮。大山鈀。三股叉。長短槌法。短兵器有單刀。單劍。雙劍。雙鞭。雙鐧。雙拐。扁担。鋤頭。雨傘。刀牌法等。共十八件。

　　最主要者。不論長短器械。要操練純熟。不但可貴為體育運動。抑亦可備為不時自衛之需也。

# WEAPONRY

It is often tauted about that anyone who wishes to practice kung-fu must first possess good character and perseverance. It is only by perseverance that one could be soft and gentle, and only through this gentleness that one could gain self-control to further achieve his goal of greatness. To the practitioner, golden words of wisdom are taught: Don't be furious over your personal enemy but fight for the people's common enemy. Don't aim for personal vengeance but root for the vengeance of the country. Be righteous, don't be afraid of hardships. Do not draw out your sword or attack at the slightest insult. For one must first learn to love his individual self, in order to be able to love his country and its people. Through this attitude, one could aspire for greatness for himself, his country and his people. This is the creed and responsibility of a real kung fu man.

In learning boxing (kung-fu), the practitioner should supplement it with weapons training. This is so because when confronting an armed opponent, he could not defend himself empty-handed. So to make him a complete fighter, a good command of various weapons available is necessary.

In ancient times, during the heyday of the bow and arrow, the different kinds of weapons are classified according to the material/substance used, i. e., either wood or metal. The wooden weapons are generally called staff. In Southern China, they refer to the wooden weapon as the club. The varying lengths of the club are 12 ft., 9 ft., 7 ft., che-bi (eyebrow's height) 5 ft. In practicing the techniques of the club, one should stand with feet in the half T-shaped, 八 shaped stance (chian-be stance). For ease, the body is twisted sideways when striking to enable the club to hit the center. This method is called the "single line body position". When holding the weapon, it should be in the chi-ngo (center) position of the body. It is very important to be exact with your stepping back and forth. By maintaining the proper forms in your right and left postures, strength will flow out naturally. With the wrong techniques and forms, strength is hindered, thus power will not come out naturally.

The techniques of the club could be roughly divided into the soft and hard methods. The upper and lower club method, the single head club, the double head club, the techniques of Emperor Sung (Sung Tai Cho) and Tamo belongs to the hard method. Master Lo Pan's method is the upper club method and this also belong to the hard method. In the hard method, you hit straight downward into the opponent's center. Quickly evade the counter attack and then counter directly like a fierce tiger descending from the mountain, your strike falling down like the downward pour of a waterfall. The power is amazingly enormous. Those who get into its path is surely destroyed. If the opponent is unable to evade the strike, he would be severely hurt or injured.

Lohan club, white crane club, monkey club belong to the soft method. In the soft method, you follow with the posture (technique) of the opponent in attacking. If attacking to the opponent's center line proved difficult, then you evade by turning from left to right. Chance upon an opening of the opponent and swiftly attack in, using the soft method to subdue the strong (hard) technique. This is the way to win. This is the meaning of the old master's advice of "thwarting a thousand lbs. with two catties". In doing the techniques of the club, be it the hard or soft method, one should always be alert in guiding the five gates of the body: high, middle, low, left and right.

The weapons made of metal are the broadsword, sword, trident, whip, steelrod, hook, etc. 双短鞭折斩馬刀

Upper X block against the horse-cutting knife

The 7 feet staff 七尺棍

## DOUBLE SHORT FLOG

The double short flog (whip) was invented by the Si jo of NGO CHO kun and for 90 years has been handed down from generation to generation. It is considered a very special kind of weapon, and is rarely seen in the kung fu circles. Throughout the province of Fukien, this weapon is very popular because it is convenient to carry. One can carry the flog inconpicously at the two sides of the waist wherever he is, making it very handy in time for self-defense.

There are four sets of forms in the double short flog and each can be practiced individually or separately against the staff (kun) or horse cutting knife (chan be to).

Ngo Cho founder Sijo uses both long and short weapons. For long weapons, there's the kwan's knife, horse-cutting knife, plum flower lance, sky's halberd, spear hook, mountain trident, long short club. As to the short weapons, there's the single broadsword, single sword, double short sword, double short whip (sai), double steel rod, double clutches (tonfa), pinta (peddler's staff), umbrella, sword and shield. The long and short weapons total up to the eighteen different kinds.

The rule to follow in practicing with the weapons, be it long or short, is to practice diligently and regularly to sharpen your skills. The practice of kung fu weapons serves not only as a good physical exercise but it would be very handy for self-defense when the need arises.

扁担廿四法　　The peddler's staff

The horse-cutting knife 斬馬刀

The beginning pose of the Monkey pole
行者棍

# CHAPTER IX - A. CHIO SO KUNG
## B. PALM STRIKING EXERCISES
## C. NGO KI ARM HITTING EXERCISES

## 石 鎖 功

### 王 安 利

　　石璜一物。練習兩臂提披之力。其功效不亞于鐵珠袋。石鎖之形式。與尋常之銅鎖無異。有鐶有壳。但無投匙之孔竇耳。以麻石或青石爲之。小者約二十斤。其大者六七十斤不等。初步專練提托。先以一手握其鐶。提至胸處。抖腕向上高舉。頻作升降。以練臂之實力。然後握鎖由下向前平提。或向旁側平提。提至鎖與肩平爲度。以練臂之懸勁。基礎旣立。則進而練翻接盤腰等法。翻接卽提鎖翻起。猛力上披。而脫手使石鎖在空中翻一轉身。或二三個身而接之。其轉身之多寡。須視臂力之大小而定。初入手不必求其多轉。蓋功夫到家之後。自不患其不熟極巧生也。待鎖轉至面前。卽舉手搶住鎖鐶。乘勢連續翻接之。前面翻接極熟之後。則練旁側翻接。側面純熟之後。更進而練頂鎖。頂鎖者卽提鎖向上拋起。待其落下時。以舉迎其居中之處。頂于拳面片刻。更撒手使鎖下墜。從上面搶接其鐶。再拋再接。初以拳頂。繼以手背頂。小臂頂。肘節頂。其法完全相同。頂鎖之術旣精。復習背花。背花有左右之別。右背花則以右手提鎖。從右腰向左肩處上拋。略扭身向左而從左肩之前面接鎖。左背花則反是。練背花使勁不可過猛。俊腦腰背各部。尤須加意照顧。偶不經意。或使力太過。鎖觸自身。每致重傷須手到眼到也。背花之後。繼習盤腰。亦分左右。右盤腰則右手提鎖從右腰處。由後轉向左脅下掉去。向左旋身而接鎖。左盤腰反是。其餘復有背花後頂接，及盤腰後頂接等法。則合二法而爲一。學者可參酌行之。以上各法。練會之後。則可易較重之鎖。如法習之。歷若干時。更接較重之鎖。自二十斤以次遞加。自能用六十斤石璜。如直條弄丸。不覺費力。則一條臂膊。至少有二三百斤實力矣。練時宜兩手互行。不必如死手功夫之專練左手也。此功成就較速。大約二年卽可告成。

# CHIO-SO KUNG (LOCK-SHAPED IRON WEIGHT)

The CHIO-SO is an iron weight shaped like the Chinese ancient lock which is used in increasing the strength and stamina of both arms. Like the metal lock of ancient China, the chio-so is rectangular, with a hollow in the upper middle portion forming the shape of a handle at the upper end of the metal. In ancient times, it is usually made of stone, ordinarily tombstone. A small one weighs around 20 kls. while a big one around 60-70 kls. The effectiveness of the chio-so is similar to the effectiveness of the "iron filling bag" ti chu tay.

There are many ways of training with the chio-so. In the beginning, practice by lifting the chio-so to chest level and then bend the arm to gain momentum and push the chio-so upward. Return the chio-so to chest level and then bend the arm to gain momentum before bringing the chio-so downward. Repeat the ascending and descending motion to strengthen the power of the arm. After this initial drill, you are now ready to proceed to the next exercise:

Hold the chio-so and lift it straight up frontally until it is at level with the shoulders. Repeat the same procedure but this time, instead of frontally, do it sideways.

Practice doing these exercises, alternating frontally and sideways. This is good for toughening the arms' muscles. Perfect these two basic movements first before proceeding to the twisting and waist embracing method.

The twisting/catching (embracing) method of chio so requires perfect concentration, timing and focus. It is not a simple exercise of upward and downward motion. This requires physical exertion since the twisting and throwing of the chio so should be done in a single quick stroke to prevent it from falling untimely to the ground. The chio so should not fall to the ground. You should be able to catch it immediately upon throwing it $360°$ roundwise (clockwise). Lift the chio so upward to shoulder leve. Release the chio so by throwing/twisting it counter clockwise with a $360°$ turn. Catch the chio so immediately upon completion of the turn. Don't let the chio so fall to the ground. Usually, a single turn of the chio so is enough. But with experts, the turn or twist may be more than one: it may be twice, thrice or even more depending upon the strength or impact of the throw and the weight of the chio so. Those who have reached the higher stages of chio so training will find out that with only one single throw or twist, the chio so may turn two or three times because of the impact of the twist. Nonetheless, the beginner should feel satisfied if he can practice with a single twist only, as this itself is already a feat. The multiple twists may come later when one has reached the proficiency of a master.

A deviation from the front throws/twists is the side throws/twists. When you have finished with the front throws, you can proceed to the side throws for greater toning and focus. You will find that the side throws is harder then the front throws since you establish focus at the sides. The hands and eyes should be keener and more alert than if you are doing it at the front. As with the front throws, you may begin by throwing the chio so in a single turn, so as to achieve balance. You can then proceed to the multiple twists depending upon the impact of the throw. The side throws is more strenous than the front. The side throws is a sort of preparation for the upward lift which is even more muscle straining than the front and side throws.

The upward lift requires more than strength and focus. Good resistance is a must here. The upward lift is done by the following: face front, hold the chio so by its handle and then throw it upward. As the chio so descends, catch it by using the back of the fist as landing port. Bounce or throw it upward again through your fist and then as it falls, receive it again at the back of your fist. If you have done this well, you can proceed to use other parts of the body like the arms and elbows for receiving and bouncing back the chio so. By the time you have perfected this movement, you are now ready to move in to the next, the back flowery movement.

The back flowery movement is practised with both hands, left and right. Here, timing and focus is very important, as you are prone to hurt yourself. With the right hand, lift the chio so and bring it backwards (for ease, twist your waist as you bring the chio so to your back). As the chio so reached shoulder level, throw it upwards overhead towards your front and grab its handle as it reached (descends) your arm level. It is important to note that you should lean or twist the body a little to the left as you are doing the right throwing technique for ease and to give an easy way for the chio so to pass. This is also done as a precaution, i.e., to establish a certain distance from the chio so and your body and the head as it (chio so) travels overhead. Repeat the same procedure, but this time, use the left hand instead of the right. In doing this exercise, the eyes, hands and body should be in very keen coordination with each other. A little miscalculation on your movements may hurt your head, waist or ribs.

The followup of the black flowery movement is the waist embracing method. Like the back flowery movement, the waist embracing method is done by both the left and right hands. Use the right hand to lift the chio so up to waist level. Swing the chio so backwards, towards your back left ribs area while twisting your body to catch the chio so with your left hand. The left embracing method is done in the same way but this time, you use your left hand instead of your right hand.

After the waist embracing method, you could further practise by combining the different movements. You could alternate the back flowery method with the upward lift or the waist embracing method with any of the two techniques.

If you have mastered the above exercises on the chio so, you could progress by shifting into a bigger and heavier chio so. It is advisable to start with a 20 kls. chio so and move gradually to a heavier chio so, maybe 30, 40 50, until you are able to handle a 60 kls. chio so. If you could already handle a 60 kls. chio so with ease, then you have mastered the methods of chio so kung and your hands by then would have the strength of 300 lbs. It is advisable to practise with both hands, unlike the other deadly hand methods like the iron palm which usually trains only the left hand. The methods of the chio so, through zealous and continuous practice, usually takes about two years to perfect.

## 五祖拳　練功法

### 石鎖功

石鎖功練習兩臂提扳之力，祖國石鎖大都用青石爲之，但菲律濱無硬石故用鐵鎖代用。

**POWER TRAINING EXERCISES**

1. CHIO SO KUNG Lock-shaped Weight Exercises

Chio-so kung is used for practising and drilling with the two arms to develop power. In ancient China, the chio-so is usually made of stone. In the Philippines, because of the inavailability of hardstone, metal is used instead to make the chio-so. The chio-so used in this demonstration weighs 30 kls.

1

2

3

第一勢
第二勢
第三勢

石 鎖 翻 接
此鎖三十公斤

### 1. Twisting-Grabbing of the Chio-so

1. Stand in a horse stance, grab the chio-so by the handle and lift it up.

2. Lift the chio-so to shoulder level; let go of the chio-so

3. twist the chio-so so that it revolves counterclockwise 360° and grab it by the handle again as it revolves back. After the grabbing the chio-so, let it swing down, and lift it up again to chest or shoulder level and twist and grab again. Repeat this sequence until you feel tired.

背花抛接

第一勢
第二勢
第三勢

2. Back Flowery Throw and Catch Method

1. Stand in a horse stance; grab the chio-so by the handle and swing it towards your back

2. As your hands go up towards your back, throw the chio so so that it flys towards your front over your shoulder.

3. As the chio-so falls in front of you, catch it by the handle. Continue the cycle by swinging your arms towards your back and throwing the chio-so again over your shoulder.

   Note:   This is a dangerous method and should be practised only after you have mastered the twist grab method. Be careful when you throw the chio-so as you might hit your head.

1

甲乙二人對拋接

| 甲拋與乙接 | 第一勢 | 1 |
| 甲拋與乙接 | 第二勢 | 2 |
| 甲拋與乙接 | 第三勢 | 3 |
| 乙接後再拋與甲接 | 第一勢 | 4 |
| 乙拋與甲接 | 第二勢 | 5 |

3. Two Men Throwing Method

1. Stand facing your partner, both in the horse stance position; lift up the chio-so to shoulder level; twist the chio-so so that it revolves 360° as you throw it to your partner (pic. 2)

3. Your partner catches hold of the chio-so as it swings towards him.

4. After catching the chio-so, let it swing down, and lift it up again to shoulder level; twist the chio-so to make it revolve 360° as it is thrown back.

5. Catch the chio-so by the handle as it swings back to you and repeat the cycle.

2

3

4

 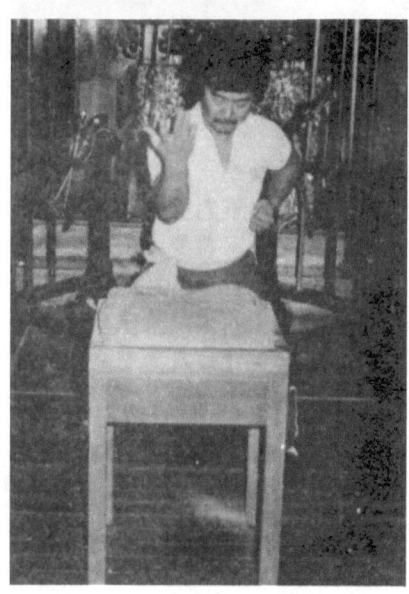

## 五祖拳　練功法

練掌功　　pic （ 1 ）　（ 2 ）

### 2. PALM SLAPPING EXERCISES

1) Stand in a horse stance infront of the sandbag; slap down with your left palm into the sandbag

2) Alternate the slapping with the front and back of the palm. Pic. 2 shows the right backhand slapping method.

1  2  3

五肢操手—專練手肢堅硬馬步靈活
（一）甲乙雙方相對，各起拳（五祖起拳五勢），然後開始
（一）甲乙雙方踏右足戰馬，右手握拳對損　　　　　第一式
（二）換左馬左手握拳對損　　　　　　　　　　　　第二式
（三）換右馬右手拳對掃　　　　　　　　　　　　　第三式
（四）換左馬左手拳對掃　　　　　　　　　　　　　第四式

### 3. NGO KI ARM HITTING EXERCISES

This set of exercises is intended for toughening the forearms and developing the agility needed in shifting the stance to an attack.

1) A and B stand facing each other; both step forward with their right leg into a chian be stance and strike their forearm with each other

2) Stepping back with their right legs, both step forward with their left leg into a chian be stance and hit their forearm

3) Stepping back with their left leg, both step forward with their right leg into the chian be stance and swing their forearm straight forward hitting them at the bony part of their forearms.

4) Stepping back with their right legs, both step forward with their left leg and swings forward with their left forearms forward hitting each other's arms.

4    5

6    7

（五）換右馬甲方走閃左畔，乙方走閃右畔右手握拳
　　　對開　　　　　　　　　　　　　　　　　第五式
（六）甲乙雙方在馬右手對挑　　　　　　　　　第六式
（七）甲乙雙方左馬右手對擒拿　　　　　　　　第七式
（八）甲方左轉身翻後過門踏左馬並左手拳開乙方
　　　同樣左轉身翻後過門踏左馬左手拳對開　　第八式

5) A step sideways with his left leg into a right chian be stance, and swings down with his right arm. B steps sideways with his left leg into a right chian be stance and swings down his right arm hitting A's arm.

6) Without moving their stances, both swing their arms upward into the open hand block

7) Without moving their stances, both A and B grab at each other's arms

8) Both A and B turn and pivot 180o to their back facing each other in the opposite direction; and hit their arms with a right hand downward block.

8

9

10

（九）甲方在馬左手挑，乙方同樣在馬左手挑　　　　第九式
（十）甲方踏右馬閃中宮右手風鼓劈乙方
　　　同樣踏右馬閃中宮右手風鼓劈　　　　　　　　第十式
（十一）甲乙雙方同時退後寄右足即寄足步招陽
　　　　手式對收拳　　　　　　　　　　　　　　第十一式

9) Without moving their stances, both swing their left arms upward into the left open hand block

10) Both A and B step backward with their left legs, and step forward with their right leg into a right chain be stance, chopping their arms downward at the middle, hitting the back of their forearms.

11) Both A and B step backward into the hanging stance and close by assuming the Chiaoyong hands closing.

# The Bible of Ngo Cho Kun

In *Chinese Gentle Art Complete*, Alexander Lim Co pours scholarship and more than 50 years' experience in Ngo Cho into the first-ever illustrated publication, and English-language translation, of this historical book on Fukien Five Ancestor Boxing. Long held as the "Bible of Ngo Cho Kun," this treatise on Five Ancestor Fist Kung-Fu has been a treasured keepsake among lineage holders of the style. Originally published in China 1917 by Yu Chiok Sam, one of the "Ngo Cho Ten Tigers," or leading disciples of the art's founder Chua Giok Beng, the book saw only a limited print run. It has been out of print for over 90 years!

This special Tambuli Media edition presents all of the original Chinese text in 244 pages, along with a new Foreword, Prefaces, an Appendix and precise English translation illustrated with over 725 clear photographs demonstrating techniques and training methods. Contents include:

- Single Short-Hand and Long-Hand Techniques
- Double Short-Hand and Long-Hand Techniques
- Kneeling and Evading Techniques
- Nine-Section Brocades
- Nine-Rotary Methods
- 18 Scholars Methods
- Solo and Partner Fighting Drills
- 38 Solo Empty-Hand Forms
- Six Weapon Art Categories

"I congratulate Sifu Alex Co for translating this rare and important book. All practitioners of Ngo Cho should have this at their side!"
—*GM Benito Tan, Philippine-Chinese Beng Kiam Athletic Association*

"Not only is Ngo Cho Kun rarely seen in print format, it is rarely openly taught here in the West. This translation is an absolute gem for Chinese martial arts enthusiasts the world over. A welcomed addition to the martial collectors shelf."
—*The Ground Never Misses*

## www.tambulimedia.com

# Kong Han Ngo Cho

Ngo Cho Kun, also known as Wu Zu Quan or Five Ancestor Fist kung-fu, is one of the most popular styles of Southern Fist in China. Currently, it is the official style of the Southern Shaolin Temple in Quanzhou, China. The founder of this dynamic art, Chua Giok Beng, had 10 disciples, each developing his own branch of the system. This book presents the core training of the Kong Hang Athletic Association branch of Dr. Lo Yan Chui, passed down and currently headed worldwide by Sigong Henry Lo, and in Canada by Sifu Daniel Kun.

*Kong Han Ngo Cho: Forms, Weapons and Fighting* begins with a historical presentation of the development of the various lines of Ngo Cho—each with a different focus on the representative systems of Tai Cho, Crane, Monkey, Monk, and Damo. The book then delves into the fundamental training that sets the basis for mastery of this style. Empty hand techniques, internal organ qigong exercises, solo forms, two man forms, training sets, fighting applications, weapon forms and applications, and full-contact lei-tai competition training are all presented in this comprehensive volume.

"A most welcome addition to the sparse reference materials on the Fukien art of Ngó Chó Kûn. I congratulate Sigong Henry Lo and Sifu Daniel Kun on a job well done." —*Grandmaster Alex Co, Beng Kiam Athletic Club*

"Kong Han Ngo Cho covers a lot of ground—most notably Kong Han's curriculum up to O-Duan—making this a most valuable resources on this dynamic art."
—*Dr. Mark Wiley, International Beng Hong Athletic Association*

# www.tambulimedia.com

www.ingramcontent.com/pod-product-compliance
Lightning Source LLC
Chambersburg PA
CBHW020354170426
43200CB00005B/173